LAST ACTION HERO ™

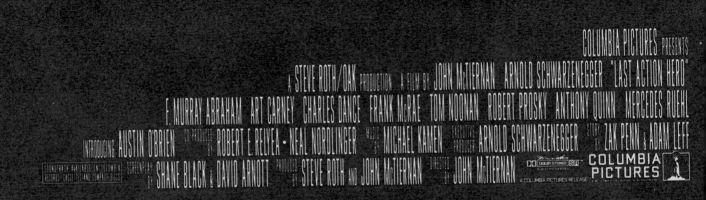

COLUMBIA PICTURES PRESENTS

A STEVE ROTH/OAK PRODUCTION A FILM BY JOHN McTIERNAN ARNOLD SCHWARZENEGGER "LAST ACTION HERO"

F. MURRAY ABRAHAM ART CARNEY CHARLES DANCE FRANK McRAE TOM NOONAN ROBERT PROSKY ANTHONY QUINN MERCEDES RUEHL

INTRODUCING AUSTIN O'BRIEN CO-PRODUCED BY ROBERT E. RELYEA · NEAL NORDLINGER MUSIC BY MICHAEL KAMEN EXECUTIVE PRODUCER ARNOLD SCHWARZENEGGER STORY BY ZAK PENN & ADAM LEFF

SOUNDTRACK AVAILABLE ON COLUMBIA RECORDS, CASSETTES AND COMPACT DISCS SCREENPLAY BY SHANE BLACK & DAVID ARNOTT PRODUCED BY STEVE ROTH AND JOHN McTIERNAN DIRECTED BY JOHN McTIERNAN

DOLBY STEREO SR
IN SELECTED THEATRES

A COLUMBIA PICTURES RELEASE

COLUMBIA
PICTURES

LAST ACTION HERO

From the story by
Zak Penn &
Adam Leff
and the screenplay
by Shane Black &
David Arnott

Steve Newman and Ed W. Marsh

The authors would like to acknowledge the following individuals for their help in making this project a fun one: Arnold Schwarzenegger for his generosity and humor; Mark Gill for for his friendship and support; Marjorie Raymond for her editorial input as assistant to the authors; David Hudson and Anders Falk, the film's videographers for their endless supply of reference materials; Sandra Murray for her patience and wisdom; Alison Savitch and Luc Nicknair for their guidance and assistance in the realm of visual effects; and the entire cast and crew of *Last Action Hero*.

Dedicated to the Danny Madigan in all of us.

First published in Great Britain in 1993 by
BOXTREE LTD. 21 Broadwall,
London SE1 9PL

Published simultaneously in the USA and Canada 1993 by NEWMARKET PRESS, 18 East 48th Street, New York, NY 10017

10 9 8 7 6 5 4 3 2 1

ISBN 1 85283 581 8

Research assistant: Forrest Wright
Book design by Deborah Daly
Printed and bound by Cambus Litho, Scotland

A CIP catalogue entry for this book is available from the British Library

Photographs by Zade Rosenthal, except as noted below:
Aaron Rapoport: title page
Barry Wetcher: 89, 90, 91, 106, 107, 118
Ethan Dubrow: 109
Luc Nicknair: 62 (far right), 72, 88, 95, 102

CONTENTS

CHAPTER
1

INTRODUCTION

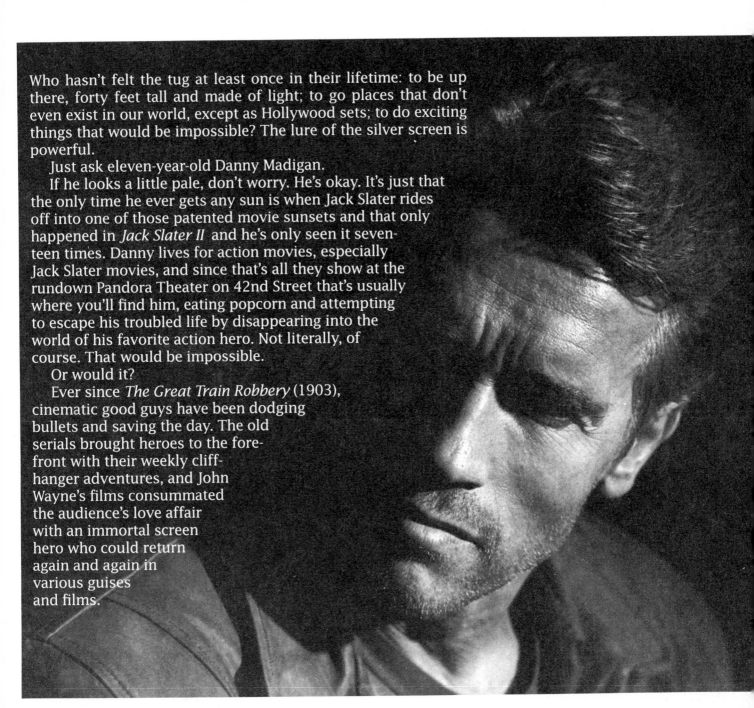

Who hasn't felt the tug at least once in their lifetime: to be up there, forty feet tall and made of light; to go places that don't even exist in our world, except as Hollywood sets; to do exciting things that would be impossible? The lure of the silver screen is powerful.

Just ask eleven-year-old Danny Madigan.

If he looks a little pale, don't worry. He's okay. It's just that the only time he ever gets any sun is when Jack Slater rides off into one of those patented movie sunsets and that only happened in *Jack Slater II* and he's only seen it seventeen times. Danny lives for action movies, especially Jack Slater movies, and since that's all they show at the rundown Pandora Theater on 42nd Street that's usually where you'll find him, eating popcorn and attempting to escape his troubled life by disappearing into the world of his favorite action hero. Not literally, of course. That would be impossible.

Or would it?

Ever since *The Great Train Robbery* (1903), cinematic good guys have been dodging bullets and saving the day. The old serials brought heroes to the forefront with their weekly cliffhanger adventures, and John Wayne's films consummated the audience's love affair with an immortal screen hero who could return again and again in various guises and films.

Who cared if he played a cop, a soldier, or a cowboy? He was the Duke!

Our movie heroes are important to us. They represent an ideal and challenge us to uphold it. It's their job.

Just ask Los Angeles police sergeant Jack Slater.

If he looks a little pale, don't worry. He's okay. It's just that his whole world has suddenly come crashing down around him. Relentless, powerful, an unstoppable juggernaut who serves up his special brand of justice one fist at a time, Jack Slater is the greatest movie hero ever to do battle on the big screen. It was business as usual—a hot pursuit from your typical dynamite-flinging hoodlums from Vivaldi's drug smuggling mob—when this obnoxious kid named Danny Madigan came out of nowhere and landed in the back seat of his '66 mint-condition Bonneville. This kid was insane. He claimed that Jack was really this world-famous actor named Arnold (what was that last name he mentioned...Braunschweiger?) and that his entire life was merely the story line for a successful series of action movies. Ridiculous! Pull the other one!

Jack Slater (Arnold Schwarzenegger) carries Danny Madigan (Austin O'Brien) into a Los Angeles police station.

8

Too bad it turned out to be true. You see, Danny knew things that no one possibly could have known, so it was no surprise when they became partners. Together they were about to crack the lid wide open on Vivaldi's racket when something impossible happened; the movie screen cracked open instead and Jack's worst enemies got away.

With Danny as his only guide, Jack must pursue the villains into our world, where a punch can mean a broken hand and a gun can spell death. When subjected to the same laws of physics as the rest of us, what good is a movie hero anyway?

Columbia Pictures' *Last Action Hero* is both a salute to and a send-up of the well-loved action genre and its undisputed king for the last decade, Arnold Schwarzenegger. Danny's journey is our journey as we follow him into this fantastic world and back again. The relationship that forms between a fictional hero and his fan is our relationship, each time we find ourselves caught up in the plot and characters of the movie.

And like every good movie…it starts with a ticket….

9

2

COLUMBIA'S MAGIC TICKET

FADE IN:

"Okay, let's roll it," says Schwarzenegger mock-impatiently as he strides onto the stage. As final adjustments are made to lights and camera, the most recognized man on the planet jokes with the film's director, John McTiernan. Seven years ago, the two men spent months covered in the mud and mosquitoes of Mexican jungles making *Predator*. In short, they are war buddies and share an easy-mannered communication that is immediately apparent to even the most casual observer. "John, the only reason we're doing this is so we can announce that we've started shooting," he smiles. "It's such a scam, I'm telling you. There isn't even any film in the camera."

It is not a scam. While nothing that gets shot today will end up in the movie, McTiernan (affectionately referred to as "McT" by much of the crew) wants to make sure that the world's number one box-office star is going to look good in tights. That's right. Schwarzenegger wears tights in his new movie.

"I know John wants to shoot some muscles, so hold on," smirks Arnold. After taking a deep breath he puts his thumb in his mouth and blows. His entire arm seems to enlarge to twice its size as his Mr. Universe muscles flex for the camera. It's an old trick for this seasoned body-builder but the crew appreciates the humor nonetheless.

The camera rolls, tilting up past high riding boots, past tights, past the delicately embroidered vest, and up to Arnold's face as he strikes a pose with a smoldering stogie. After an actor's moment of deep introspection, he speaks. "To be or not to be."

That's right. Schwarzenegger plays Hamlet in his new movie. McTiernan calls cut and stands motionless, eyes closed, chin in hand. The crew waits. Those who have worked with the man before clue in the rest as to what is happening. McT is thinking. Notorious for his ability to stand undisturbed in the middle of total production chaos, the director is trying to see something in his mind. After a moment his eyes open, and he smiles at one of the assistant directors. "Do we have any of those Terminator sunglasses?" An assistant is dispatched. People smile. The wardrobe test is getting silly.

"LIKE WINNING THE LOTTO"

Long before those cameras rolled, in the summer of 1990, novice writer Zak Penn found himself asking a question: "What would happen if a kid got sucked into a movie and used his knowledge of genre to make his way through it?" The answer? Adventure. Together with his partner Adam Leff they set out to create a story with all the trappings and clichés of the action genre, an amazing and dangerous playground for the character that would become Danny Madigan. The time was ripe for parody. As McTiernan would later point out, "A number of people have decided that as long as they have the predetermined number of explosions and muzzle flashes they're doing it right. They've just made fat targets of themselves because once you

try to paint-by-numbers the audience catches on."

Penn and Leff submerged themselves in the genre, studying scripts and videos with the fervor of two scientists in search of a secret formula for the ultimate action hero, Jack Slater. Producer Steve Roth remembers, "In the first draft, they named him Arno Slater, so it was pretty obvious who they were aiming for." Even so, the team made sure the work would stand on its own, knowing chances were slim Schwarzenegger would even read the finished screenplay. As new writers there was no way to get the script in the door. Until they employed Slater-style ingenuity and just knocked it down. Using friends who were assistants they bombarded agents all over town with copies, saying "Have you heard about these guys? Have you read this script?" Within a week they were signed. Within two weeks, Columbia Pictures executives had purchased the script. "There were nine out of ten passes on the project," explained Roth. "Everybody, except for Columbia and Mark Canton, figured it was going to be impossible to get Arnold, and without him the movie wouldn't have been even half as good. There's Arnold and then there's everybody else. Getting Arnold was like winning the lotto."

BIG GAME HUNT

Columbia Chairman Mark Canton likened the project to a big game hunt with a summer blockbuster their intended prey. Together with head of Production Michael Nathanson and Executive Vice-President Barry Josephson, he convinced Schwarzenegger to consider the project. "Once committed, Arnold immediately involved himself in the development process," said Canton.

Schwarzenegger was impressed. He wanted to give the script to the best action writers in the industry, to build it up, make it funnier, and insure that the action sequences of the movie-within-the-movie were as wild as they could possibly be. "Then," Schwarzenegger felt, "the writers needed to show what action and violence is like in the real world to create the contrast and make it powerful."

Enter Shane Black and David Arnott, who were asked to work with grace under pressure. Recalled Barry Josephson, "They were writing against a ticking clock. If Arnold was gonna do this as his next movie, we had to have a script ready pretty quickly."

The writers, like McTiernan, looked forward to poking fun at their chosen field of expertise. "What we hate about action movies is that so many of them are just energy releasing itself in the forms of explosions and/or broken elbows," said Black. "What's been forgotten is the idea of suspense. Setting up a scene so that you want to find out what happens next." They strove to push conventions, such as car chases and shoot-outs, several levels beyond the expected.

The team was also given carte-blanche to come up with some of the film's funniest scenes, often at Schwarzenegger's expense.

KILL-ZINGERS

"Quick! What's a good line?" asked Penn and Leff as they searched for the perfect phrase Jack Slater could toss out as his calling card. They had narrowed their search to fifty phrases, before choosing one offered by Zak Penn's girlfriend: "Big mistake." Little could they know those three syllables would become the foundation of Slater's no-nonsense vocabulary.

Black and Arnott wanted a catch phrase too, something to use as a running joke. Arnott asked Arnold what he called the repeatable phrases and was surprised to find out that they had no name. "I started to call them *killzingers*," Arnott enjoys recalling. "We'd spend a couple of hours coming up with nasty killzingers to see if we could find situations in which to use them. It's really hard to come up with good ones. At one point we had Slater killing someone in a church and Slater says to the priest, 'Don't worry, father. I'm making him more holy.'" While Black and Arnott did create some absolutely gut-twisting puns, good taste prevailed and "Big mistake" became to *Last Action Hero* what "I'll be back" is to *Terminator*.

They picked on his accent. ("What accent?") They picked on his previous roles. ("Alien in the jungle?! That sounds horrible!") They even picked on his name. "When Jack asks Danny how to spell Schwarzenegger, he replies, 'Don't even try it.'" Black laughed, "It's such a wonderful image to have Arnold unable to say his own name, let alone spell it."

Not all of the jokes came from the writers, however. "We wrote a scene in which Schwarzenegger and his wife, Maria Shriver, show up and do some jokes together at the premiere," explained Arnott. "But obviously that's such a rich environment that once you've got Leeza Gibbons asking the questions, Arnold's going to have fun with it. I mean, how many actors would agree to make fun of their own marriage just for a good laugh?"

BRINGING THE MONKEY TO NEW YORK

After the Black/Arnott draft was completed and Arnold committed to the picture, there was still the matter of fleshing out the characters and themes. Schwarzenegger knew what he wanted: "The action hero has to teach Danny something about life

because he really has no life at all, yet. At the same time, Danny has to teach Jack about the real world, about the fact that even though he's a fictional character he can still be a real hero."

It was apparent that for the script to succeed the cardboard action hero would have to be capable of growth. Writer William Goldman was brought in to finish the job. He compared the story to King Kong: "It's great to go into the jungle and see the monkey, but the story doesn't start until the monkey comes to New York." Goldman hammered out the humanistic changes Slater and Danny would go through in the real world, subtle events creating something greater, such as Jack's sudden interest in classical music, or the the revelation that Jack is actually very lonely in the movie-world. "It's a relationship movie in a nutty sense," confided Goldman. "I hoped to make them vulnerable so that when you think Slater's going to die, you're moved."

It had taken five writers and countless others more than two years to create a screenplay that would go before the cameras in just a few weeks. The time-line had been pushed to the limit as the crew spent the last few days getting ready for the five-month production juggernaut that was about to begin.

"Actually, it was that short window that really forced us to know what movie we wanted to make," observed Canton. "You don't want to make an in-between movie with Arnold. You want it to be the next big film."

Playing themselves, Arnold Schwarzenegger and his wife Maria Shriver attend the premiere of Arnold's latest action picture, *Jack Slater IV*.

15

3

UNSTOPPABLE

NO SURPRISES

"Helluva way to spend Christmas," says Police Lt. Cornelius Dekker, a tougher-than-nails tower of a man who absolutely does not want to be at Lincoln Elementary School. The Ripper has taken fifth-graders hostage on the roof. Helicopters circle the three-sided brownstone, which stands out like an impenetrable monolith amidst the one and two story structures of Culver City.

Actually it's not Christmas, though thousands of decorations emphatically state otherwise. It's November 2nd, 1992, the first day of production, and cast and crew are hard at work finishing the movie. *Jack Slater III*, that is—the movie-within-the-movie that begins *Last Action Hero*.

If Lt. Dekker is tougher than nails, however, then Sgt. Jack Slater is the hammer.

Schwarzenegger is about to make a classic movie entrance onto the scene by striding purposefully across the tops of sixty police cars—just as soon as stunts finishes marking out his path with strips of slip-proof bathtub tape. (His rattlesnake-skin boots may look cool, but they're slippery as can be on these metal rooftops. "Can't have our star end up with a concussion on the very first day, now can we?" quips Brian Cook, the Australian assistant director.) At the moment it looks as if Arnold is floating on a sea of red and blue flashing lights, as his torso obscures the last letter of a sign creating the somewhat prophetic sounding statement, "JOHN'S HARDWAR." John McTiernan probably couldn't agree more. First day of production and already weather has reared its ugly head, heavy winds forcing them to abandon the scene on the roof early, putting more stress on the overstressed production schedule.

Big deal. It's still gonna be fun.

The three-sided building was erected in the 1920s for stars working on the nearby MGM lot. When McTiernan explored its triangular rooftop with production designer Eugenio Zanetti,

A production sketch of the elementary school from the film's opening scene.

they fell in love with the place. The perfect setting, they said, for the final confrontation between Slater and his arch-enemy, The Ripper. The production crew was less than convinced. "There was nothing that said school or danger," explains Carl Goldstein, assistant director. "You looked out and for three hundred sixty degrees there was nothing."

But that was eight weeks ago when there was nothing.

Literally nothing.

With script rewrites still coming in regularly, the proverbial ball had finally started rolling and eight months of preproduction were compressed into two.

"There were no surprises. On a big picture like this there can't be," explains line producer Robert E. Relyea. If there were such a position as "on-set dad," Relyea would fit the bill. Years of experience lend him a calm and trusted judgment that is reassuring to cast and crew alike. "It simply meant that we prepared as we went. We knew the first two weeks of shooting and that was enough for everybody to fall in line."

Costumes were designed. Sequences were storyboarded. Coffee was consumed. The work first started to take on a visible shape, color, and form in the art department where Zanetti and crew concocted strange visions of an alternate movie-world California where anything was possible, including a Californian elementary school shaped like a New York brownstone. It was not uncommon for weary individuals to make late night pilgrimages to the sketch-filled halls in search of inspiration and focus before going home to collapse.

The Ripper (Tom Noonan) terrorizes a group of young hostages on the rooftop of the elementary school.

Now the drawing has become reality, lit beautifully by director of photography Dean Semler and crew. Construction arms surround the rooftop like curious dinosaurs, carrying spotlights high into the air to simulate an unending procession of police helicopter traffic. Periodically everyone is bathed in an overpowering blue brilliance, their distinct shadows thrown onto the Santa Monica Mountain range miles away. The mundane has become magical.

Zanetti's most noticeable contribution to the set is the Santa sleigh rising away from the chimney with its eight electric reindeer. Never mind the fact that the entire roof is a set built on top of a real roof. The fake roof is user-friendly and safe for the fifth-grade extras, with removable heating ducts, higher railing, a false drop-off for the Ripper's demise, and inset skylights, which allow Semler to bottomlight The Ripper in the classiest of monster-movie traditions. The only disadvantage Zanetti cannot overcome is the roof's size. Its standing-room-only size forces crew members into the one corner not seen by camera. Meanwhile, McTiernan works with the children, getting them to scream convincingly as The Ripper looms over them with his ax. It becomes a game as the kids turn their shrieks on and off while McT directs the symphony. Hands up SCREAMING. Hands flat silence....Everyone is ready to shoot.

Too bad Santa Ana winds are blowing everything to pieces. Santa's sleigh starts to vibrate dangerously, threatening to pull off its mount. Dust and pollution stings everyone's eyes, especially Tom Noonan's, who's wearing special contact lenses to make his eyes jaundiced and bloodshot for his role as The Ripper. The production has no choice: lose the minors early and start the scenes that take place on the ground where the wind can be controlled.

"Background action!" Three hundred swat men start maneuvering in and around the cars. "Action, Arnold!" The boots trudge forward now, stepping from roof to roof confidently, a mere walk in the park for this action hero.

McT is using a long lens, which means Arnold's journey forward will look even cooler with all the lights stacked up together, the boots the only part of Arnold we see until he clears the last car and drops down into frame, his face set with the grim determination of a man who knows there's an ax at his son's throat. Like the script tells us, "Jack Slater is in a bad mood tonight."

Next shot. Steadicam, following in front of Slater as Lt. Dekker tries to stop him. The sixty police cars Arnold just walked on are cinematically "recycled" by pulling them farther down the street for Arnold to pass a second time. The two men rehearse as the Steadicam and its operator follow along in front. Dekker shouts after Arnold. "You go in there and it's your badge!" On that cue, Slater is supposed to casually toss his badge over his shoulder without breaking stride and Dekker is supposed to casually catch it. The rehearsal is perfect.

"Oh, no! We should have rolled," laughs Arnold. "Now we'll never get the badge toss right again!"

Nine takes later, thankfully he is proven wrong.

Hearing of the hostage crisis at the school, Jack Slater (Arnold Schwarzenegger) arrives on the scene and soon takes matters into his own hands.

4

PERFECT BUDDY MOVIE MATERIAL

"I'm Slater's new partner. Jack and I will be working together for the duration of the film."

As Danny Madigan, Austin O'Brien got to live every kid's fantasy playing opposite his favorite movie hero, Arnold Schwarzenegger. "He's big!" exclaimed O'Brien. "He's an action guy even in real life."

In the beginning of the movie, Danny's having trouble coping with life in New York City. His mom is always at work, and he has no real friends his own age. "He's more of a wimp than I am," admits O'Brien about his character. "He's been mugged a couple of times and he's afraid his life isn't going to change any. And it helps him to go see his action hero, because it makes him feel like, 'This is the guy who I wanna be like when I grow up.'"

Blasted out of his movie seat, Danny had to become an "action guy" himself to meet the challenges of the mile-a-minute

Danny Madigan (Austin O'Brien) finds himself caught up in an exciting chase to catch the bad guys, but realizes, too late, that in this picture he's the comedy relief!

An early production sketch depicting an original idea as to how Danny would land in the movie. The effect would have involved building a revolving set that, when tilted, would appear to drop Danny into the screen.

(Below) Danny tries to prove to a bruised and beaten Jack Slater that they really are in a movie.

story: dangling high in the air off a gargoyle in a rainstorm ("It was kind of hard, but it was still very fun.") to playing chicken with some killers ("I'm the comic relief! This isn't going to wooooork!") to making a movie in New York ("There are NO laws in New York! Everybody just swerves around making up their own lanes.") Austin proved himself to be the perfect buddy material for Arnold and this action-packed movie.

According to McTiernan, "We expected it to take months to fill the role, but as soon as I saw Austin, I said, 'Yep, there he is.' Most preadolescents have the ability to concentrate on make-believe without getting distracted or embarrassed, but Austin has that ability mixed with some pretty good technical skills, too. It makes him ideal for this kind of movie."

Action hero Jack Slater (Arnold Schwarzenegger) protects Danny Madigan (Austin O'Brien) from two of his world's most dangerous criminals.

Those technical skills would be further honed by acting coach Mike Muscat, who helped him prepare for the more emotional scenes and encouraged his natural abilities. "Austin's got great comic timing, and I think that comes from having a photographic memory. It allows him to relax and play with something instead of just worry about saying it right. That's a big plus, especially when you're dealing with someone as dead-on in their timing as Arnold."

Schwarzenegger was quick to adopt the boy and his family on the set, helping Austin to relax and be himself in what can sometimes be a very stressful environment. Between takes they would play Hot-Hands, "where you put the other person's hands on top of yours and you try to flip yours over and slap them," O'Brien explained. The dynamic duo would also make merciless fun of each other's flub-ups. "There was this one time where Arnold's supposed to say, 'Rescue the virgins from the top of a

25

burning building,' and instead he said 'Climb the building and save the burning virgins.'"

"I was cracking up because he wasn't this stuffy young thespian, he was this honest-to-goodness eleven-year-old," laughed assistant director Carl Goldstein. "You can forget that sometimes when you're dealing with child actors."

O'Brien's playfulness eventually rubbed off on the crew. "I started a silly-string fight with him, which was a major mistake," confessed stunt double Peter Kent. "He came back and nailed me with it, so I got four cans, chased him into his trailer and his mother came out chasing me with a can. It ended with a huge silly-string war in the parking lot."

Making a movie is certainly fun for a kid but it's not easy. O'Brien gave up most of his Saturdays, which meant sacrificing Little League, among other things. "Also, I have to do double shifts of acting and school every day." Three hours each day O'Brien studied in an intensive one-on-one relationship with Pia Mehr, his on-set social worker and teacher. "It's difficult for Austin sometimes because things can become so intense on the set that he has trouble switching gears when it's time to learn," said Pia. Even so, O'Brien never fell short of his motto, "Be cool. Stay in school." The young actor even expanded his homework to in-

The camera crew films insert shots of Austin O'Brien that will later be edited into the film's "dynamite chase" sequence.

clude learning German. When he finally surprised Arnold with it, the Austrian was proud of the boy's efforts.

That wasn't exactly the case when O'Brien displayed his vaudevillian gift of mimicry on Arnold's accent, explained Muscat. "Arnold caught him doing it and immediately started correcting him and giving him pointers! It was hilarious." With the privilege of learning from the master, O'Brien's impression was soon so polished that the script was revised to include lines for Austin with the Arnold accent. (Imagine Schwarzenegger speaking one octave higher and you'll get the idea.)

Austin had another effect on the script, one that Columbia Pictures wholeheartedly supported in it's desire for the film to be released PG-13. "After this film comes out I think I'm going be seen as a role model for some kids, so I don't want them to think it's cool to swear. I've cut out the cusswords as much as I can. There's a couple that are part of the story, but since they make a point about cussing, it's kind of okay."

Relatedly, O'Brien feels that the story of the film has a positive message for young people that comes through in the choices his character makes. "When Danny finally feels what it's really like to hold a gun I think he sees it's like, kinda scary. Violence is scary. In the movies it's different, but in real life, it's not the answer."

O'Brien's favorite scenes didn't involve big guns, big laughs, accents, or even big stunts. True to his open personality, it was when "Danny really becomes Jack Slater's partner," O'Brien shared. "It's in the middle of the movie and they're talking about their dads and how Danny lost his to cancer. And Jack just puts his arm around Danny. I think that's a really great scene."

With shooting completed and Little League still weeks away, what were his plans? O'Brien grinned. "I'M GOING TO PLANET HOLLYWOOD!"

5

LAST ACTION HAMLET

While the rest of *Jack Slater III* is left to second unit, McTiernan and crew travel to Denmark to start work on the now infamous Hamlet sequence. Fortunately, Denmark is a mere seven blocks away, waiting on Columbia soundstage number 15 where Zanetti has created an Elsinore castle of Arnold-sized proportions.

"I didn't quite realize it was going to be so big," comments McTiernan during a preliminary walkthrough. Crossing the functional moat, the drawbridge leads you under a deadly-looking portcullis, and then you go down a regal stairway and into the central chamber, a cavernous space lined with thick stone pillars like ancient tree trunks. Medieval drapes and tapestries fill out the interior, hiding the fact that other chambers are merely painted backdrops. At the far end, a two-story stained-glass window casts sunlight into a small chapel. Fans of classic movies may find this portion of the castle familiar; it is a stone-for-stone replica of the chapel from Laurence Olivier's production of *Hamlet* (1948).

"*Hamlet* was made when there was almost no money in England, so they had very little to work with. We wanted our set at least five times larger than that," says Zanetti. "I merely built around an image John McTiernan had suggested. 'Isn't it great to see a man riding his horse up a staircase?' he asked. 'Isn't that a powerful image?' So I built it large enough for the hero and his horse and that dictated the grandness of everything else. And, since we only had to match that small portion of the chapel area to make the transition between the two films work, why not have some fun?"

Why is *Last Action Hero* trying to match Olivier's *Hamlet*, anyway? Isn't it a movie about an LA cop in the 1990s? Such questions nagged studio employees for weeks as they passed the set-in-progress on their way to work.

Elsinore Castle is the setting for an elaborate daydream. Danny has just arrived late to his English class, fresh from the screening of *Jack Slater III*. His teacher is trying to sell her students on the idea that Hamlet is not only Shakespeare's greatest

play, but literature's first action hero. "Ghosts! Sword fights! Sex! And in the end everybody dies! Shakespeare's *Hamlet* couldn't be more exciting!" she explains, rolling a clip from the Olivier version. Needless to say, Danny has his own interpretation of what it means to be an action hero and Hamlet, with his wimpy tendency to philosophize instead of fight, just doesn't cut it. As the pensive prince stands over the praying Claudius, Danny decides that it's time for a little rewrite...

(Above) Danny's English teacher (Joan Plowright) teaches the class about Shakespeare's *Hamlet*.

(Below) *Hamlet* as imagined by young Danny Madigan with Jack Slater (Arnold Schwarzenegger) in the starring role.

Setting up a shot for the *Hamlet* sequence on the cemetery set. The sequence appears in back and white with computer-generated color added to highlight certain elements in the design.

INT. ELSINORE CASTLE—DAY

Back in Elsinore, Claudius still prays at the altar.

Hamlet, however, looks a little different. He's still got the black turtleneck, the gold medallion, but his BACK, his SHOULDERS…they're huge.

The Prince emerges from the darkness, and hey, this isn't Laurence Olivier…it's Jack Slater. And he looks ticked off.

> SLATER
> Claudius. You killed my father.

The deep voice from the trailer kicks in:

> DEEP BASS ANNOUNCER
> SOMETHING IS ROTTEN IN THE STATE OF DEN-
> MARK…

SLATER HOISTS Claudius OFF THE GROUND.

> SLATER
> Big mistake.

> DEEP BASS ANNOUNCER
> AND HAMLET IS TAKING OUT THE TRASH!!!

33

SLATER chucks Claudius out the STAINED-GLASS WINDOW. Colored shards follow him down to the raging waters below.

"That was my brother's idea," explains writer Zak Penn. "We had a scene where Danny is watching *Hamlet* in school and my brother came up with the 'Something is rotten' line as an action 'tag' for a movie trailer and it was perfect. It was really inspired, so we ran with it."

On set, McT studies two video monitors, one showing the original film and the other showing the "video tap" image from his camera. The images match perfectly if you ignore the fact that one of the two Hamlets clenches a cigar in his teeth.

"Big mistake." Arnold pushes the actor playing Claudius off the small box which makes him look like he's being held up by the lapels of his kingly garments. Cut. Three takes in and Mc-Tiernan still isn't happy with the camera move, a 180° dolly which starts on Hamlet's back as he approaches Claudius and ends on an intimidating close-up of Hamlet-as-Slater administering his special brand of justice. The shot must work as the transition between Olivier's version and McTiernan's, so the camera move is crucial. Plus there's a question of performance. Should Slater toy with his prey or be dark and brooding in his vengeance? How would eleven-year-old Danny imagine it? And lastly, there's the matter of "business"—the little actions that help punctuate a particular line of dialogue or performance. When should Arnold light the cigar? And when should he close the Zippo lighter with the sharp one-handed snap of a man with a mission? These and other seemingly insignificant decisions will either help or hurt the comic timing of "the moment" and are discussed at length by actor and director. "That's obvious, John," says Arnold in a knowing voice after McT makes a suggestion, "I mean, I have studied Shakespeare." Two takes later, McTiernan is happy. The move is perfect. The performance is right. Now for the stunt.

A tiny hole is drilled through God's yellow halo—through the stained glass, that is—allowing a thin cable to be threaded into the set. It is attached to a harnessed Claudius and the other end is married to one of Lane Leavitt's patented stunt devices. Owner and operator of Leavittation Inc., Leavitt has specialized in safe ways to make stuntmen fly through windows, fall off buildings and otherwise defy gravity. While this rig may not compare with some of the monsters he will concoct for this film, it will provide Arnold with enough super-human strength to hurl a man thirty feet through the air. On cue, Arnold throws Claudius as Leavitt triggers the pulling mechanism. The combined forces fling the murderous king through the window, crashing onto the thick stunt pads piled up outside.

ONE STUNT DOWN, ONLY *263* TO GO.

With no apologies to the bard, the Hamlet sequence is structured as a spoof of the adrenaline-pumping "coming attractions" trailers that have heralded the release of every action picture ever made. Thus, McT isn't concerned so much with creating great scenes as he is with getting great shots. And the crew has been encouraged to go all out.

Going all out actually started weeks before, when Arnold met with stunt coordinators Joel Kramer and Fred Waugh and weapons trainer David Walling to choreograph a number of melees between Hamlet and the guards of Elsinore castle. "The one thing John doesn't want is little fancy moves like Zorro, you know?" explained Arnold, demonstrating traditional fencing maneuvers. "None of that tack-tick-tack-tick kind of stuff. He wants really powerful moves. Two handed moves, just chopping people down, like whummm!" The sound effects added to the power of his strokes. The small wooden practice sword looked truly deadly as he wielded it Conan-style through the air, with both arms swinging in slow motion. As the four men blocked out a routine for the first time, Arnold led with the wrong foot, quickly finding himself open to an attack from Kramer. "I'm telling you, one false move and you're history. I love this kind of stuff."

On set, the routine is executed flawlessly. It looks much better now that they're fighting in costume…almost. Designer Gloria Gresham has done a meticulous job recreating the Olivier costume in every detail from head to foot, but since the camera won't see his feet Arnold has opted to remain in tennis shoes, creating a strange contrast with his medieval garb. Make-up and hair masters Jeff Dawn and Peter Tothpal have resurrected

Hamlet, starring Jack Slater (Arnold Schwarzenegger) as envisioned in the daydreams of young Danny Madigan.

Arnold's Terminator look (stern features, short spiked hair), making the contrast even stranger.

The shot is an attack by three guards, ending with Hamlet slicing through a tapestry to reveal Polonius, who tells him that they've taken Ophelia hostage. As they rehearse, McT picks up a broadsword to demonstrate. "Arnold, all that sword fighting in Conan was compressed and rooted," McT demonstrates by clasping the sword hilt near his chest, "and the one way I've never seen you photographed is open and dynamic as opposed to just physically strong." Arnold agrees. This time he performs the maneuvers one-handed, leaving the other arm free to counterbalance the force of his swing like a lethal ballet. The open approach works much better. "We've run out of excuses. Shoot it."

Brian Cook, first assistant director, has been busy staging other melees in the background so that when the camera rolls the cavernous set fills with the muffled sounds of several cinematic battles. The three attacks come off flawlessly, but when Arnold slashes at the tapestry, a small snowstorm of feathers explodes in his face, desperately too late. McT keels over with laughter. Peter Kent calls to Arnold. "You killed a chicken?" (Tommy Fisher's effects crew has overdone the feathers just a touch.) Arnold is so amused that he asks to see playback twice and its even funnier to him the second time.

"There is no stopping this madness. We're totally out of control!"

The sequence only gets sillier.

A decidedly different version of Shakespeare's *Hamlet* starring action hero Jack Slater (Arnold Schwarzenegger) as dreamed up by Danny Madigan.

As shooting continues over the next few days Danny's imaginary Hamlet racks up an impressive body count. Castle guards come at him in ever-increasing numbers, like medieval Keystone Cops, only to be cut down by his sword, thrown twenty feet into solid stone walls, or mowed down by his Uzi 9mm.

Uzi 9mm?! Sure it's a stretch, but what the heck! He used a Zippo lighter in the first scene, didn't he? This is a kid's daydream, remember? Even poor Yorick's skull can become a weapon if thrown with enough force ("Heads up!"). As the gags escalate, so do the references to other movies. Arnold walks Terminator-like down the corridor, automatic weapons firing from both hands. As guards cross the drawbridge, Rambo-Hamlet rises from the misty moat, ready to take them out from below. In one shot, Arnold improvises a line of dialogue mid-take before skewering a hapless guard with his broadsword. "I wanted to add one of the Predator lines...'Stick around.'" In the end, the prince rides up the castle stairs on the back of a regal black horse, victorious. All that's left is the traditional big action movie-trailer finish—blowing everything up!

While it may seem unnatural for the production to invest such tremendous amounts of time and effort into what is essentially an extended gag, consider what it accomplishes for the story. First, it establishes Danny's wild imagination and sense of humor, proving he's a worthy partner for Jack in the movie-world. Second, in an indirect way it introduces the themes Jack Slater will have to deal with in the real world. "To be or not to be" is truly our fictional hero's deepest existential dilemma, regardless of whether he's wearing tights at the time. Third, it's a hilarious vignette that playfully pokes fun not only at Arnold's career within the action genre, but at the action film's traditional opposite—the "art film," whose supporters so often seem to snub everything that isn't "cultural."

Most important, however, it provides us with a crucial clue as to just how weird *Last Action Hero* is going to get. Up to this point in the story nothing out of the ordinary has happened. Nick won't reveal the magic ticket for several scenes. Watching Schwarzenegger on screen as the pistol-packing Prince of Denmark reminds us that, to paraphrase the immortal bard, there are stranger things on Heaven and Earth…and in the movies…than are dreamt of in our philosophy.

6

Q&A WITH ARNOLD SCHWARZENEGGER

When asked to describe Schwarzenegger's off-camera personna, associates are quick to point out that what you see is what you get, a charming man with a zest for challenges and a confident focus on the task at hand.

Because Schwarzenegger is the heroic movie icon of our time, *Last Action Hero* would have been pointless without his total involvement. "Everything he does brings good will to the public," says Mark Canton, "and that manifests itself in his tremendous worldwide following." The secret to his success? Directors and producers agree: Schwarzenegger never takes himself too seriously. And on *Last Action Hero* he's letting the audience in on the jokes...

Q: How would you characterize the tone of the film?

A: In a way, *Last Action Hero* is a spoof on the stereotypical aspects of action movies. It shows "inside" the movie and how tough movie heroes are: how they never have to reload their guns, how they climb walls, fall from highrises and never die; how they always win and the bad guy always loses, and so on. Then you see a hero come out into the real world, and you find he's just a normal human being who can't have all those adventures. What I think makes it really work is that since I've done so many action movies in the past, now I can make a spoof. It is satire, but at the same time it tells an interesting story about a child being sucked into the movie and becoming part of the life of his favorite action hero. So we also see everything through Danny's eyes as he rides the rollercoaster and goes through this "wonderland" kind of thing. I thought it would be great fun to watch if it was directed properly. And for all of us, the number one choice was John McTiernan.

Q: Could you describe what the magic ticket does?

A: Danny goes to endless amounts of action movies, and his favorite action character is Jack Slater, played by me. Spending

that much time at the theater, he's become good friends with Nick, the projectionist, who invites him to a special private screening of *Jack Slater IV*. And he gives him this beautiful old ticket, claiming it has magic powers. Maybe it'll do something crazy, maybe it won't do anything. Who knows? So he's watching my movie, and a big car chase starts to happen on screen. I'm talking major action, with explosions and crashes and fire and one of the bad guys throwing dynamite at my car. I use my expert marksmanship to change its course mid-flight. What I don't notice is that it flies out of the movie screen and lands next to Danny. What Danny doesn't see is that the ticket is glowing in his pocket. Boom! Danny goes flying into the screen and lands in the back of my car. That's when he becomes part of the adventure.

Q: What made you and McTiernan feel that Austin O'Brien was right for the role of Danny?

A: When you have a child in such a big role it is extremely important that he acts in the most realistic way possible. That can be very tricky. A lot of times a child actor acts too professionally. His performance loses the special innocence of the child. I went through this on *Terminator 2*, where we tested a lot of child actors and most were too pretentious or too well trained, and you could really sense it. On this one we were fortunate enough to find Austin O'Brien, who has done a few things but not too many. So he brought a very instinctive and improvisational quality, while still possessing the necessary acting skills to work a scene and improve on it and at the same time not look like he was acting. It's a difficult thing to do. Austin was the only one, I think, who really felt the emotions and brought the kind of realism that we needed to his performance.

Q: Could you describe the two worlds we are going to see?

A: The important thing is to contrast them. And we do that through Danny. Danny points out all the inconsistencies to Jack and tries to prove to him that he's not real. But for Jack, it's all real. As far as he's concerned he's this LA cop who can climb an eighteen-story building on the outside and rescue two virgins, who can jump a speedboat over the Santa Monica Pier at eighty miles an hour and land on the merry-go-round and get the brass ring embedded in his forehead, only to have it healed up two minutes later. It's just his life. He's never thought much about it. He even tells Danny, "I'm involved in all these crashes and explosions. I jump out of airplanes, but I keep surviving!" He's amazed by it all, but he just feels that it's luck. Danny tries to convince him that some "schlemiel" in Hollywood is thinking up all this stuff and the only reason Jack's not dying is because he's the most popular movie action hero in Hollywood. He can't die. They need him for sequels! *Jack Slater XV, XXIV,* and so on!

He's not very successful in the beginning. But then something goes wrong, and the bad guys escape into the real world using Danny's magic ticket, and we have to follow them. That's when I realize that yes, I have been in a fantasy world. And now, when I try to do the same kinds of action, nothing works. I see the criminals driving away, and I tell Danny, "Here's another explosion for your movie, kid." I shoot twice and nothing happens. In my world the bullets would have hit the gas tank and blown up the car instantly. Here, they just leave two little holes and that's it. Later on, I run out of bullets. That's never happened to me before. Danny tells me, "This is the real world, Jack. Here we have to reload guns." He starts teaching me about the differences.

Jack Slater (Arnold Schwarzenegger) distracts the gun-toting mourners at a Mafia funeral and makes off with the body of the explosive Leo the Fart.

Jack Slater drops in to surprise a couple of thugs.

John did a fantastic job shooting the two worlds different ways. The real world is New York, where it's raining, dark, lonely, and depressing. Movie world is California, where it's sunny, palm trees are everywhere, the ocean is incredibly blue, and the women are perfect "tens," you know. It's all about contrast.

Looking for Arnold Schwarzenegger movies in a video store in Jack Slater's world, Danny Madigan (Austin O'Brien) is amazed by what he sees.

Q: This movie is rated PG-13. What kind of statement do you think the film will make to young people?

A: Most of my movies are made to entertain people. But if there just happens to be a statement, then it's great, and I think we have one of those situations in this movie. It shows this action hero doing crazy stuff on the screen, including a lot of over-the-top violence. When he gets out into the real world, however, he gets hurt fast. He realizes what effect guns and explosives can have. He learns what a devastating effect violence can have on real people. He realizes that the lifestyle of action and violence that he's been used to for so long is really the wrong way to solve problems, that as a police officer there are other ways to go about helping society.

That's really why I consider *Last Action Hero* a spoof of action

45

movies, because on the screen it's fine to run around shooting people and blowing up so many things that it becomes ridiculous, because it's just fantasy and fun. It looks good on the big screen. In reality, however, its no way to live. It's no way to handle yourself or to protect yourself or solve problems, basically. That's the message we've brought into the movie through the characters and what happens to them.

Q: When you were a boy, who were some of your favorite movie heroes and where would you go if you had Danny's magic ticket right now?

A: When I was a kid, I thought Kirk Douglas did some of the most terrific westerns. Or John Wayne and Marlon Brando. And the women of course, Elizabeth Taylor, Sophia Loren, Marilyn Monroe, and women like that. I admired these people. I would always see the movie when I saw their names on the poster. Now, as an adult, if I had Danny's magic ticket, I'd like to learn a little bit more about the "wild west," or Viking times maybe. I'll

be doing a movie soon about the Crusades, so I'd like to step into a historical movie like that to learn and feel what life was really like back then.

Q: How was it working with John McTiernan again?

A: I learned to respect John during *Predator*. He has tremendous talent, and he's done a great job directing this movie, not just in terms of the suspense and the action but also in terms of the comedy. He himself is not a funny guy. He's very dry. Very low-key. And when you first meet him you ask yourself, "He can do comedy?" But he's incredibly good at creating situations that make you howl with laughter. Artistically he's matured a lot since *Predator* because he's directed so many more movies. He did *Die Hard* and then *The Hunt for Red October* and things like that. And each movie has revealed different qualities. In this one he's putting them all together. Also, I feel I've grown as an actor since *Predator* so I think we work together much better now than we did back then, even though our working relationship was great back then, of course.

Q: Why is Jack Slater the last action hero?

A: He's unlike anyone else. He's the biggest box-office draw. He's the most successful action star. There's no one else like him around. He's the last of his kind....

CHAPTER
7

THE BEST OF TWO WORLDS

Anthony Quinn holds a stubborn thumb high in the air. "Vivaldi is number one!" At first, there is nothing particularly noteworthy about his delivery.

Then you notice the statue behind him. It is, perhaps, the least ludicrous element in this self-aggrandizing Italian mansion that is Vivaldi's home. It stands in tribute to the greatness of Rome, hand raised in a noble gesture. McTiernan compares the hand to Quinn's own proud thumb and makes a decision. That afternoon, the statue has been altered to ape Quinn's gesture.

Such is the magic of movie making.

In addition to plaster thumb surgery, *Last Action Hero* presented production designer Eugenio Zanetti and costume designer Gloria Gresham with an opportunity to quite literally design two movies in one: the movie itself and the movie-within-the-movie, *Jack Slater IV*. The common thread between the two is young Danny, blasted out of a real world he cannot handle and into a fictional world he knows by heart—the Wizard of Oz in reverse.

WORTHY OF THE ADVENTURE

At the intersection of those two worlds stands the Pandora Theater, a time machine where decay and magic are locked in eternal battle. Nick tells Danny that he once saw Houdini perform there when he was a kid, back when the Pandora was a vaudeville house. "I wanted it to be a magic place," explains Zanetti, "even if it belonged in the real world of this dreadful rundown New York, because the story needed a doorway worthy of the adventure about to happen. I can remember how truly magical movie palaces used to be. Newer generations have lost that." Using the historic Orpheum Theater in downtown Los Angeles, Zanetti populated its aisles and lobbies with paintings, statues, gargoyles—paraphernalia not so much of 20th-century cinema but of 19th-century theater, harkening to the memory of Houdini and other magicians long dead, their dark arts mixed

49

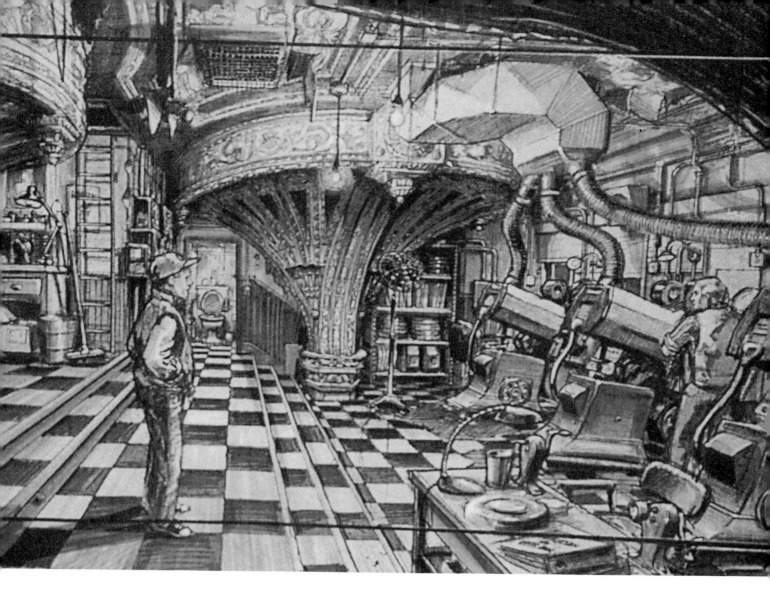

A production sketch of Nick's projection booth at the Pandora Theater.

somehow with the dust dancing in the projector's beam.

Hidden within its walls was Nick's home, the projection booth. Designed as a movable "cover" set that could be taken anywhere, Zanetti's hope was to create a refuge for Nick, a gilt and granite cave for the storyteller where the giant pillars and arches of the Pandora's ceiling reach in and join, like the arteries of a giant heart. "He's this mad opera designer," exclaims McTiernan of Zanetti, "it just takes a while to catch on to which opera he's designing!"

At the Pandora, McTiernan made a point of trying to include the art deco EXIT signs in certain shots as a visual reference for the audience to know where they were. But to which exit was he referring?

OUT THE DOOR...

"It's the world that we all happen to live in," says McTiernan, explaining his approach to shooting so-called reality. "Time is

Nick (Robert Prosky) is fast asleep in his projection booth at the Pandora Theater.

continuous and therefore nowhere near as exciting as in a movie, because getting from point A to point B doesn't happen in an instant. You can't edit life. Plus things don't happen as neatly as we'd like."

Or in Danny's case, things don't happen neatly at all. An innocent, Danny is defenseless against a vicious and indifferent New York which the writers describe as a gauntlet of dealers, junkies, and hookers. On 42nd Street, that description was made real when the design team resurrected porno shops and re-lit theater marquee's that had been dark for years with titles like *I Want Your Blood* and *Your Blood or Mine,* a partial parody of the pointless movies McTiernan had wanted to take to task. Life on 42nd Street is no church picnic by any stretch of the imagination, but Zanetti's additions emphasized the sordid side and Gresham's costumes fed into the hopelessness.

"New York is not a world that's human-scaled anymore. It's a world where man means nothing. And certainly for a little kid growing up without a father that would be tremendously stressful," said McTiernan.

51

Action Hero Jack Slater (Arnold Schwarzenegger) hits it off with Danny's mom (Mercedes Ruehl) when he spends time in the real world.

WINDEX FOR THE WINDOWS OF THE SOUL

For Charles Dance, production design didn't stop at his white linen suit and assassin's pistol. It literally stopped in his left eye. McTiernan wanted the villain to express his many moods with an eclectic assortment of glass eyes. "Have a nice day," he says coolly to Slater, pulling down his sunglasses to reveal a classic 70s' smiley face where his left iris should have been.

"I have quite sensitive eyes," admitted Dance, "and the thought of putting bits of plastic in them filled me with more than a little apprehension." Lens designer Richard Snell created a small "eyebrary" of the scleral lenses that were gentle enough for Dance to wear for extended periods of time. When not in use, they were stored in tiny vials like exotic lab specimens.

Each eye presented a different challenge. As make-up supervisor Jeff Dawn re-called, "There's so little space opened up in the eye that you have to make everything much tinier than you would think. We ended up with an itsy-bitsy smiley face which on a forty-foot movie screen comes across as quite large." Strong simple graphics worked best, like the concentric circles of a bullseye, or the number on an eightball. More than half a dozen different designs appear in the movie, several of which were surprises to the director. "The most fun Charles had with it was when he'd expose a new lens to the director for the first time," said Dawn. "He'd start a conversation with McT and at just the right moment pull off his sunglasses. Usually, John went 'Wow, what an interesting lens. Let's use it!'"

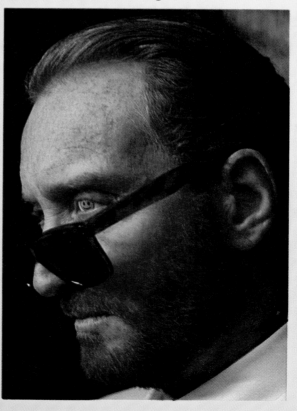

Built to ridiculously tiny proportions, Danny's apartment epitomized all that is dispiriting about the city. Schwarzenegger barely fit into the kitchen. "You had to take one wall out," recalls Zanetti. "That kitchen was maybe five feet square and when you put three people in there with a camera and everything, it really illustrated the difference between the two universes."

THROUGH THE SCREEN...

Nowhere was the design team's creative energy more apparent than when creating the land beyond the screen, the colorful world of fictional heroes and villains that is Jack Slater's Los Angeles. With sets like the police station, the rooftop funeral and Elsinore castle, Zanetti recognized "a chance to appeal to the purity of a child's imagination and the massive imagery it can summon forth." Armed with a staff of four art directors, a half dozen illustrators, a score of set designers, and more than five hundred carpenters, they set about their work.

Using illustrations, cardboard models, complex computer-simulated environments and a persuasive (if heavily accented) tongue, he and director McTiernan mapped out what Slater's Los Angeles would look like. The contrast in their two approaches was summed up by one of the assistants: "McTiernan asked for a set and Zanetti delivered an entire world."

Zanetti's wild imagination was driven by his interpretation of the movie as a fairy tale appealing to the positive aspects of human behavior. "In terms of that world, Arnold's character represents the mythical hero. His persona shapes the world that he inhabits." Thus, everything was built and tailored to the hero's bigger-than-life proportions, often dwarfing young Danny quite comically.

A production sketch of the entrance to the Los Angeles police station.

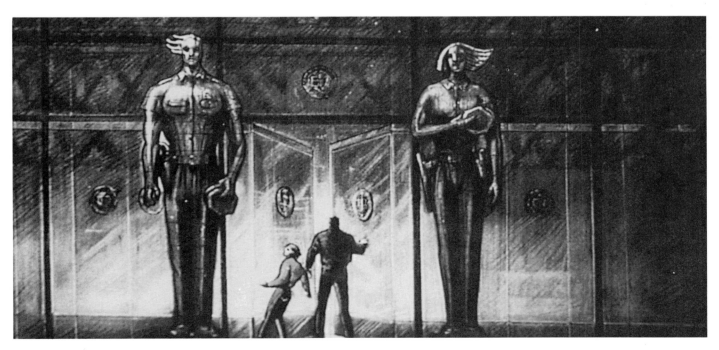

53

McTiernan remembers, "Zanetti's first design for the police station was 760 feet long. There wasn't a soundstage in the U.S. long enough to build it, so Eugenio insisted that we move everybody to the former Czechoslovakia to build his set. I'm only half kidding."

In the end, the police station was shot as a dressed location in the appropriately named Filmland Building in Culver City, with a lobby stretching an impressive 780 feet, surpassing even Zanetti's expectations. In contrast to the drab and empty station Danny visits in New York, the movie-world station is totally awesome. The desks and chairs look like they're on loan from the Deathstar. Laser beacons shoot information through the air. Thirty-foot granite statues tower in tribute over the men and women in blue. The walls are real, but everything between them has been created or put there by Zanetti and crew.

For Costume Designer Gloria Gresham, the station was a chance to be outrageous. She and her staff populated its corridors with the motliest crew ever assembled—from robowomen

Inside the Los Angeles police station in Jack Slater's world.

cops dressed in Thierry Mugler outfits featuring chrome breastplates to midget motorcycle gangs, to Hare Krishna cops—the overwrought precinct bordered on total absurdity.

"I was proud of myself," recalls Carl Goldstein, in part responsible for the eclectic extras in the station. "I'd added this group of shriner extras in purple fezzes that had been arrested with these weird prostitutes. John absolutely hated it. He said, 'It's too far out.' I said, 'Too far out? You've got an animated cat walking around.' But he was right. He focused the humor. Didn't make it too silly." McTiernan walked a critical line between silly and absurd, for fear that his audience would become distanced from the characters and their plight. "Afterwards, whenever McT'd say 'put a fez on it,' we'd know we'd gone too far."

McTiernan tailored his direction to match the exaggeration of story, costumes, and sets that defined the movieworld. "Everything is shot with long [telephoto] lenses, bringing the interesting elements into focus and eliminating the boring details. It compresses more action into the frame. The most exciting bits are done in slow motion. And every character is a giant figure photographed from slightly below because everyone needs to look like he's six-foot-eight. And moment-to-moment reality is completely manufactured by edits. In essence it's all a giant illusion, this grand fabrication up on a movie screen."

(Above) Some of the colorful characters that occupy the Los Angeles police station in Jack Slater's world.

(Below) The camera crew sets up a shot with Arnold Schwarzenegger and Austin O'Brien in the Los Angeles police station.

High Rise Farewell

But the biggest fabrication was up on the roof of the Long Beach Hyatt, where the design team of *Last Action Hero* created a set for the most outrageous Mafia funeral in film history. Work began by x-raying the existing roof and figuring out just how much wild stuff could be added up top. Then, in a truly gargantuan feat of engineering, hundreds of carpenters built a five-level terrace running the length of the hotel, complete with cascading waterfall, glass atrium, and functional exterior glass elevator. As

all the elements came together they were covered in bright red formica and finished with gold trim.

"Color is like music; it's doesn't go through the intellectual eye. One simply feels it," explained Zanetti. "So since we muted colors in the real world we wanted a strong color statement to constantly remind us that we're in this hyper-reality." Zanetti and Gresham agreed that the color should be red. It was vibrant, it had impact, and in a strange way it hinted at the dangerous, amped-up nature of this action universe.

Again Gresham's team added to the look by dressing the

(Above) Jack Slater (Arnold Schwarzenegger) hears an ominous sound emanating from the body of Leo the Fart.

(Below) The mourners take aim at Jack.

59

mafia extras as wildly as possible. "We knew it would have to be black mostly, but we didn't settle for plain black suits and dresses. We gave everybody a wild hat or an exciting tie/shirt combination...something slightly eccentric to match the eccentricity of the set." (The only extras who dressed relatively normal were the nuns and priests, but the propmaster made up for it by making them carry bigger weapons.)

While the rooftop scenes were enjoyable to prepare, they were incredibly difficult to shoot. After five years of sporadic rainfall, southern California was suddenly experiencing its longest uninterrupted stormfront in decades. Nicknamed "The Great Drought-Buster," storms pelted the

(Opposite, above) Jack Slater is surrounded by gun-toting mobsters at a Mafia funeral when he attempts to abscond with the body of Leo the Fart.

(Opposite, below) Slater drops the corpse off the roof and onto a waiting crane.

(Right) John McTiernan (far right) rehearses a Steadicam shot with his two stars.

(Below) Danny Madigan (Austin O'Brien) desperately tries to maneuver the crane.

coastline for weeks, wreaking havoc on the set. Every inch of rain that accumulated on the temporary rooftop translated into thousands of pounds of additional weight, forcing crews to squeegee water all during the day to prevent collapse. The red formica tiles warped and cracked. Two weeks of shooting turned into three.

During this time, the crew often found refuge on its main cover-set, the projection booth, which had been carted down to Long Beach and erected in the former home of the Spruce Goose, a cavernous dome, dwarfing the tiny set.

"Then one morning," as Bob Relyea recalls, "the rain had stopped temporarily, and we went up to shoot a sequence on the roof only to find the glass elevator missing. After a while somebody noticed it on the ground over three blocks away. A tornado had ripped it off the roof!"

(Above) Setting up a helicopter shot through the elevator for the rooftop sequence.

(Right) Strapped into a middle body harness and suspended by two thin cables, Schwarzenegger's descent is controlled with the same kind of brakes used in automobiles. Anything less could not be trusted and situations like this don't leave room for second chances.

DRESSING THE LAST ACTION HERO

While designing the hero's world was a massive undertaking, deciding what that hero would wear was no less daunting. Gresham drew on movie history for inspiration. "Originally the picture was called *THE Last Action Hero*, so I was thinking about how I could put into one outfit the synopsis of everything, the whole genre of cinematic heroes." Gresham traced its roots back beyond Douglas Fairbanks to the cowboy films of Tom Mix and William S. Hart. "It was a look Arnold had never used on film before, which was western boots and jeans, the belt buckle and the jacket. It's a little Mel Gibson, a little Nick Nolte, a little Stallone, but it does have a definite western feel to it." To contrast the sharp straight lines of Arnold's character, Austin was given the look of a street kid, clothes too big and never tucked in right. Standing beside each other, the two characters almost did look like they belonged in different worlds.

"It's interesting that the real world was seen as New York, and the fictional world was pegged as Los Angeles, but that's how most people see it anyway, I guess. We did our best to accommodate that," smiles Gresham.

Both Gresham and Zanetti credit their crew for making it through the fast-paced schedule. "Some people worry and complain and moan about how hard the work is," says Zanetti. "They're the ones who learned that tension and attention were the same thing. It doesn't have to be that way and the crew was great. I'm ready to make another movie when I should probably rest up in a hospital some place, actually."

JACK'S JACKET

When Slater's leather jacket design was finally nailed down, the costumers cranked out several more identical copies. "You need them for the stunt doubles," Gresham explained. "Plus it's a movie-fantasy so the clothes are always clean and wonderful no matter what happens to them. He oozes out of the tarpit, wipes his face off, and magically his jacket has returned to its pristine condition." (The one coated with goo is dispatched to an emergency dry-cleaner.)

Gresham noted that there were other uses for the unique wardrobe. "Arnold is very smart. He's made enough movies to know that costumes can become very valuable once a film is released. And because he's so generous with charities he keeps the clothes; not for himself, but to raise money." While the film was still in production, a pair of Schwarzenegger's Tony Llama boots were auctioned off for thousands of dollars to raise money for the Magic Johnson Foundation for AIDS research. "And that's just one pair of boots," enthused Gresham. "When it's time to auction off these jackets he'll be doing a lot of good in the world, bless his heart."

8

EVERYTHING WENT BOOM

November 24, 1992

On the corner overlooking downtown Los Angeles rests a beautiful little yellow house with white trim. At least, that's what it looks like from the front. As you travel downhill, the house and its two neighbors quickly give up their secret—they're phony!

"IT'S A BOMB!" Slater comes tearing out the front door, followed by two uniformed policemen. A FLASH! Slater flings himself dangerously off the porch as the tongue of a fireball emerges on his heels…

…and stops. Arnold lands in the fluffy stunt pad. "Much better!" McTiernan is very pleased with the timing. "Arnold, it was great. You jumped off the porch and behind you everything went boom. We got it."

Assistant Director Brian Cook picks up the megaphone. "Moving on!" In this instance, moving on means setting up a much wider shot for a much bigger explosion. Painters clean up all evidence of the little blast while stunt coordinator Joel Kramer positions air ramps on the porch. These compact pneumatic catapults will send the stunt doubles through the air, as if thrown forward by the force of the blast. Kramer will be doubling for Arnold in this second stage of the explosion and is wearing Jeff Dawn's Schwarzenegger prosthetics. His lips barely move under the makeup, which causes one onlooker to mistakenly assume he was the victim of bad reconstructive surgery, but boy, isn't he lucky to have ended up looking so much like Schwarzenegger so he can do stunts for him!

Inside the house, special effects coordinator Tommy Fisher and his crew rig metal flashpots for the second largest explosion they will create today. The pots will instantly incinerate powdered peat moss, creating a larger, controlled fireball aimed at Kramer and the other stunt doubles, motivating their parabolic flights off the porch.

The crew, however, is only slightly interested. Like jaded

NO
PARKING
10 AM to 12 NOON
WEDNESDAY
STREET CLEANING

spectators at a Fourth of July fireworks show, they're waiting patiently for the finale. The script has promised a destructive fireball to rival any Joel Silver action epic you care to name and they know Tommy Fisher's crew can deliver it. The second stage goes off without a hitch, stuntmen flying through the air almost ballet-like as smoke and flames erupt behind the door and windows of the little house. When they land, the grass ripples unexpectedly. (The greensmen had buried stuntpads under the sod.) And now it's time for the big one.

Bright orange primer cord snakes in and around the wooden supports inside the house, coiling around posts and over doorframes. Triggering that alone would turn the place into splinters. For the fireball, special cannisters are rigged with gasoline and black powder charges. Up on the roof, a man scores long breaks with a chainsaw so that the fireball will have some place to go, pushing chunks skyward. "You can control the size of an explosion pretty well. On the big ones it's the direction that can get a little tricky," explains effects assistant Scott Fisher. "But since gas ignites and dissipates pretty quickly, there won't be much danger as long as everyone's a safe distance away." Blending intuition with generations of experience, Fisher is sending the blast upwards and outwards, the horizontal force dissipating itself across an empty lot. If all goes well, a mushroom cloud of flame and jet-black smoke will

eclipse downtown Los Angeles, leaving nothing of the house standing. At the same time, it must force a police car to flip over backwards, a feat which will be accomplished by triggering an air mortar rigged under the engine compartment. The car is also anchored to the ground with thick cabling so that it can't land on a camera or go flipping end over end down the hill and into traffic.

From his cellular, a policeman calls command posts. Without doubt the upcoming blast will generate calls within a ten-mile radius and the production doesn't want any surprise visits from firetrucks—they've brought their own.

Meanwhile, McTiernan and director of photography Dean Semler set cameras. Lots of cameras. A three-story platform is erected for the master angle. Others are trained on the police car, while others are anchored to the ground in crash housings very close to ground zero. All of them will be triggered remotely.

As the moment approaches, the assistant directors must fight to send the crew all the way across the street. "The fire marshall was insisting that we shut everybody down except for camera," explains Carl Goldstein. "It was ridiculous. Everyone was hiding behind cars and trees because they didn't want to be that far away. They wanted to see the big boom."

No one more so than production designer Zanetti. "We build sand castles so we can stomp on them. The little kid in all of us wants to see things blow up. And when my production design-ing friends see the movie they will realize what a beautiful little set I created because you can't do these things to real houses. The owners tend to get upset."

At 12:10, everything is set. Two-hundred-plus crew members line the street, looking back at the house. At this distance, they see the explosion before they hear it, chunks of roof spinning skyward, flames obliterating everything. When the shockwave reaches the crew, it cracks a one-inch plate-glass window be-hind them. The fire marshall wasn't kidding.

All told, the production will pay for forty or so broken win-dows in the surrounding neighborhood, a bargain given the fact that everything went off without a hitch and on schedule. Line-producer Bob Relyea remembers the elated moments right after the explosion. "There's always tension because it's a one-shot deal. And when everybody was rushing back in to check cam-eras and so on, I turned to John in excitement and said, 'Well, how'd you like that?' And he turned to me, 'I think we need to do it again.' Then he cracked a smile and I knew that he'd kept his sense of humor through the whole thing."

Calls to police stations numbered in the hundreds. A few had seen the blast, but most wanted to report an earthquake. Every-thing's fine, folks. Just Arnold Schwarzenegger making his new movie.

9

THE FLYING TRUCK

The goal? Catch Benedict. The obstacle? A thick wall between Jack's monster truck and Benedict's living room. No problemo, right?

Actually, it's more complex than that. Jack and Danny must crash through an outside wall, fly over the second-floor balcony and land the truck on all four wheels in the atrium of Vivaldi's mansion, literally "getting the drop" on Benedict.

The problem? This plush Malibu location just happens to be somebody's cherished home and Schwarzenegger is not about to leave gaping holes in someone else's house. It's not polite. And then there's that annoying detail about trucks being launched from second-floor balconies rarely landing on all four tires. The solution is surprisingly simple.

Later on, the truck will crash through a fake set-piece built to match the mansion. For now, the truck will be lowered into the atrium from a special cable rig. This only leaves one problem. The truck is three times larger than any of the available entrances.

Enter Tommy Fisher and his special effects squad. They are about to perform the ultimate college prank and get paid doing it. They're about to take the truck apart piece by piece and reassemble it inside the house. "Will chunk by chunk do?" Fisher smiles as his crew lights up its blowtorches.

To provide a sturdy anchor to hang the truck from, an aluminum framework designed for concerts has been assembled inside the atrium, its bulk hidden behind plants and other set dressing. Reassembled without its engine and looking only slightly the worse for wear, the truck is rolled into position and two steel cables are attached to the frame through holes in the body, one in front, the other in back. Fisher gives the "up" signal and the truck, a powerful beast with monster tires, rises into the air about one foot. Now, the effects crew must balance the vehicle to the weight of Peter Kent and Danny's double, Bobby Porter. And let's not forget Benedict's stunt double, Charlie Brewer, who must sit at the bar with his back to the action as everything comes crashing down around him.

Nobody wants to do this twice. Every camera will roll.

Slowly, the truck is wenched high above the marble floor, revealing the effects crew's final touches—air cannons mounted near the ceiling, stuffed with bits of plaster and drywall.

With the truck dangling menacingly above their heads, denizens of the art department struggle to move their pièce de résistance into place. Weeks ago in a forgotten meeting, someone asked, "What if the truck were to land on a statue of Vivaldi and crush it like the foot in Monty Python?" That question has blossomed into an answer as a life-sized plaster statue of Anthony Quinn's Vivaldi character (with the stubborn thumb) is hefted into position in the middle of the room.

Everything is ready. Cameras roll. "Action!" Air cannons explode. The cable rig snaps taught with frenzied power. One pulls the truck inexorably forward, while the other two send it falling towards its untimely rendezvous with the sculpture. Something goes wrong.

In the middle of its descent the truck veers violently to the left, threatening to dump the stuntmen out the side. Kent, professionally calm, tries to make it look like he's steering to correct the problem, but physics have taken over. Then the front wheels kick over the statue with a mighty shove. Its eight hundred pound torso skids in the direction of Charlie Brewer who, as of yet, does not know anything is wrong. His first clue comes when Vivaldi's plaster head rolls between his legs and shatters against the wall like a bowling ball fired from a cannon.

Whitney's truck dangles menacingly above the crew at a plush Malibu location.

Even then he does not flinch.

As the dust settles and the cameras cut, the statue's main torso rests inches from Charlie's back. Everyone is fine. In fact, the only casualty is the truck, which sags in the center of the room, it's rear left wheel buckled under. Kent takes it in stride. He turns to the nearest camera and with a mock British accent calmly states, "It's so hard to find good parking spots these days."

An analysis of the video playback reveals the problem. The rear right tire clipped on the corner of a cast-iron elevator railing, sending everything rolling. The shot will have to be reset and performed again after lunch.

Later, Kent congratulates Brewer for his grace under pressure. It's a good thing his back was turned, he says, otherwise he might have freaked.

"Are you kidding?" laughs Charlie, "I saw the whole thing in the reflection of my drinking glass. For a split second I thought you guys were landing on top of me!"

10

THE FACES OF LAST ACTION HERO

Arnold Schwarzenegger is JACK SLATER!!! decrees the forty foot billboard overlooking Times Square. But who the heck is everyone else? "This is the first time I've had so many famous people from the acting community interested in doing my movies," recalls Arnold. "It was great because it made me feel like we had a real winner of a story." Familiar faces mix with newcomers in what is surely the largest ensemble cast in Schwarzenegger's career...

PANDORA'S LAST MAGICIAN

Actor Robert Prosky was the Danny Madigan of his generation. "I'd sit through *Robin Hood* three times, if I could, until my mother convinced the theater owner to go in and find me." More than fifty years later, it is fitting that such a lover of movies should become Nick, the projectionist of the old Pandora Theater.

Dressed in an authentic-looking 1920s' usher's uniform, Prosky rehearses with Austin for the camera, holding out the as yet untorn ticket in his fingers. "This is a magic ticket," he begins, soon enthralling Austin to the rhythm of his words. The magic isn't in the ticket. It's in the performance.

MERCEDES RUEHL

Like Danny, Mercedes Ruehl looked to the silver screen for inspiration at a young age. "I spent the better part of age nine or so imitating Katharine Hepburn in *Morning Glory*, much to the distress of my family!"As she was steadfast in her ambition to become an actress, her performances went from basement to Broadway, Tonys and Oscars supplanting the praise of relatives.

As Irene Madigan, Ruehl plays a woman fighting the daily pressures of single motherhood in the Big Apple. Is it any surprise, then, that super-hero should fall in love with super-mom? "I think they were hoping to convey the pleasant, delicate, and delightful kind of relating that only happens between men and women when they're slightly enchanted with each other." Mind you, this happens for like two seconds in the movie! Making Slater stand still long enough for coffee, conversation, and Mozart, Ruehl's character does more than her share in rounding out the two-dimensional action hero.

LETTING OFF SOME STEAM

Frank McRae is really a very quiet man. You wouldn't know it when you see him towering over Slater and Danny, spewing forth a bilious outrage worthy of Mt. St. Helen's volcano. While his throbbing migraine and steaming ears come courtesy of the makeup department, his PG-13–rated tirades are a delicate combination of writer's ingenuity and performance.

"I put it all together in what I call gibberish-jive," said McRae. "If you could slow your VCR down, you might notice a bad word, but most of the time it's this wild stuff the writers came up with." (What does he mean when he calls Slater a "ball-peen jack-amenace"?)

"I'm almost sure it's English," wisecracks Danny.

A simple yet effective trick adds a hilarious result to Frank McRae's performance.

Anthony Quinn (left) as Tony Vivaldi threatens Slater's cousin Frank (Art Carney).

"THEY KILLED HIS SECOND COUSIN... BIG MISTAKE"

He's not quite dead yet. Ironically, Art Carney proved that he's still kicking in his death scene opposite Schwarzenegger. By the time his parting gasp finally sputtered to a stop, the crew was rolling on the floor with laughter. The two actors had worked together once before.

"I was in Arnold's first television appearance," remembers Carney. "It was a Lucille Ball special and Arnold played a body builder/masseur. Now look at him. He's got more money than I have!"

ACTION GIRL OF THE NINETIES

"She's just like him," smiles Bridgette Wilson, the dynamic young actress who plays Whitney, Jack Slater's daughter. "She likes karate and target practice. You know, the feminine things every girl wants to do."

The Whitney character is a new addition to the Slater universe, one that is welcomed by young Danny. (He's fallen in love with her picture on the lobby standee.) Does this mean spin-off movies like *Whitney Slater: Prom Queen Undercover*? As long as there's an occasional cameo by the original Slater, you never know. "He's the real action hero. And he's a great film dad. Not bad at all. I'll take him."

And let's not forget our villains...

AX HIM NO QUESTIONS...

LEEZA GIBBONS
What are your plans for this evening?

THE RIPPER
I...I thought I might kill someone.

To accept actor Tom Noonan's description of The Ripper as "a heavy metal guy who's looking for a good time" is to call Hitler kind of kinky. "The makeup does a lot of the acting for you," the actor explained. "If you just walk and talk you can't help but look menacing." It took three hours in the chair each time the actor needed to be transformed into Jack Slater's arch-nemesis.

When he wasn't slinging axes at Arnold or throwing youngsters off of rooftops, Noonan was sharpening his directing skills, cutting an independent feature of his own. Not bad for a twice-dead ax murderer. (Film students take note.)

DANCE WITH THE DEVIL

VIVALDI
Meet Mr. Benedict. The genuine article, you better believe it. Benedict can take you out easy as cake.

BENEDICT
(to himself)
Easy as pie, you Sicilian schmuck.

Why is Benedict, a superior villain in every respect, putting up with this two-bit mafia don? "To put a roof over his head," explains actor Charles Dance of his character's laconic attitude. "Plus, it gives him the opportunity to kill people which is what he really likes to do. He considers himself the crème de la crème of villains and he's just standing in the wings to make his entrance into the world of villainy."

It was the dark humor of the role that attracted Dance. "Unlike a lot of Hollywood villains, he has been written with great wit. Antagonists tend to be rather dreary, but because of the nature of this story, characters that start out two-dimensional reveal more dimensions as the film progresses."

Dance took the clichés of the action genre in stride. "I quite like the villain's gun running out of ammunition. Bang bang bang...click. There's plenty of mileage left in that yet." Benedict has more than a few surprises up his sleeve for Jack Slater.

But it is the fantasy of the magic ticket that has most inspired Dance to play the low-life of a lifetime. "It's the essential ingredient in a lot of successful movies. When this ticket comes into his possession, nothing is impossible."

The actor gets a demonic smile on his face...
"Irresistible, isn't it?"

IN LIKE QUINN

Though the man Anthony Quinn plays is a garish, half-witted Sicilian mafioso with a tendency toward malaprop, nothing could be farther from the truth in real life. The career of this two-time Academy Award winner has taken on the shadings of legend. "He's the answer to a great trivia question," explains co-star Charles Dance. "Who has appeared in more films than any living actor? Answer: Anthony Quinn." In this movie, quietly intelligent Quinn gets a chance to exercise his funny bone, playing the dim bulb in charge of LA's largest crime syndicate.

VIVALDI
Benedict, what is this? One minute you're my friend, then you do a total three-sixty on me.

BENEDICT
One-eighty, you stupid spaghetti slurping moron. One-eighty! If I did a three-sixty I'd go completely around and be BACK WHERE I STARTED!

VIVALDI
(long pause)
What?

PRACTICE MADE PERFECT

DANNY
Watch it, Jack. He killed Mozart!

In a departure from his Oscar-winning performance as the jealous Salieri in *Amadeus,* F. Murray Abraham relished playing John Practice, FBI agent and 'Nam buddy to Slater. If that sounds like a clichéd combination, think again. "To suggest it's a cliché sounds like you know what to expect. You can't," intimates Abraham. "The clichés are the basis from which the surprises spring."

Does this mean that John Practice isn't a backstabbing two-timing long distant cousin of court composer Salieri? Abraham smiles: "I'm a good guy in this film…maybe."

HEY, ISN'T THAT…

McTiernan wanted to populate the hyper-reality of his fictional Los Angeles with as many famous faces as possible. Tina Turner plays the Mayor of LA in *Jack Slater III.* On set, she let it slip that she hadn't seen Arnold's latest film. Arnold was shocked. "I don't believe this. You don't watch my movies? I sure watch your legs!"

Some cameo's were blatant references to other movies. Cop-seducer Sharon Stone (*Basic Instinct*) and cop-copier Robert Patrick (*Terminator 2*) appeared in the wild LA police station where Slater and every other movie cop in the known universe seems to work, regardless of whether they're living, dead, or even animated.

While Joan Plowright isn't as recognized, the value of her cameo was in its subtlety. As Danny's teacher she tried to interest the MTV generation in Sir Laurence Olivier's *Hamlet*, only to be terrorized by paperwads. "This proper English actress was defending herself against real grade-schoolers. McTiernan was in tears," recalled assistant director Carl Goldstein. How many people will recognize that when Plowright sang the praises of *Hamlet* she was also singing the praises of her departed husband, the great Olivier?

"The premiere scene was ideal for cameos," recalled Arnold, "because each person would add legitimacy to the fact that this was a real premiere. We had Chevy Chase and Tony Curtis, Hammer and Tori Spelling; had about twenty big names walking through and talking to Leeza Gibbons and Chris Connely about their favorite Jack Slater movies. It was wild. And they wanted to do it!"

On the day planned to shoot the sequence, fifteen trailers had been ordered, an entire limousine company had been put on hold and special makeup personnel had been called to active duty. Bob Relyea recalled, "At exactly the appointed hour, thirty limousines and one helicopter pulled in from all over southern California." Jean-Claude Van Damme. Little Richard. Jim Belushi. Damon Wayans. "It was a field day for these people."

Months later, McTiernan sat at the editing table with a sheepish look on his face. "I have a dirty secret. A lot of them have been cut out. Time reasons." Such is the way with cameos—the movie must come first, a fact you can bet the stars who participated understand better than anyone. As the old saying goes, "There's no such thing as a small role…only small actors." On *Last Action Hero*, there were certainly no small actors of any sort.

Tina Turner as Mayor of LA.

(Above) Joan Plowright.

(Below, left) Sharon Stone watches the monitor with stars Arnold Schwarzenegger and Austin O'Brien.

(Below) Robert Patrick plays a cameo as the evil Terminator, the T-1000.

C H A P T E R
11

"WE'RE IN NEW YORK?"

THE LITTLE BIG APPLE...

The view would be splendid if it weren't for the rain, which pelts down on the crew as if banished from heaven. Times Square is lit up for the world premiere of *Jack Slater IV.* Arnold himself is going to be there. You can almost see his black Humvee with gold trim (the "formal dress" version) on Broadway when...

"Save the rain, Tommy!" The downpour is suddenly gone, as if turned off at the spigot. As you look at Times Square now without the instant weather you start to see things. Like the fact Broadway and Seventh Avenue are a translucent backdrop wrapped a full 270° around this rooftop. That the lights you thought were Arnold's car are actually a series of delicate fiber optics simulating traffic. That the rooftop is resting on a wooden platform some forty feet tall and that the other "buildings" are two-dimensional and warped somehow as if designed by Salvador Dali. Close one eye (like a camera) and the truth reveals itself; everything has been built in forced perspective, creating a much larger looking space than would be possible on a soundstage, even Columbia's biggest soundstage, Number 27.

More than fifty years ago, Munchkins welcomed Dorothy to Oz on this stage. Later Gene Kelly danced in his galoshes. Now it's Mr. Schwarzenegger's turn to sing in the rain as he spins his little daughter in his arms and croons an off-key version of the Kelly classic. It is between takes and Arnold is trying to keep the crew's spirits up despite a ghastly work environment. Actor Charles Dance (from England and therefore an expert on rain) sums it up best: "Special FX rain is the wettest rain in the world. Three seconds of that dreadful stuff and you're soaked completely through." To make it worse, portable furnaces heat the source water (for the benefit of the actors), turning the whole place into a big steaming greenhouse. Camera lenses fog left and right. The fatigue of the heat and humidity is overwhelming. Bob Relyea recalls, "There was a twenty degree difference

from the top of the set and the bottom, and another twenty degree difference between the bottom and outside where there was a terrible storm. With a situation like that you're inviting people to get down."

Philosophically, this set shouldn't even exist. "The challenge," explains Zanetti, "is that it has to look like you're really in New York or you break the real-world premise of the movie." Rain helps the illusion. Camera placement does the rest. The decision to even attempt this massive deceit was based on control, since stunts and special effects were crucial to these climactic scenes. Plus, temperatures in New York this week are averaging -10° F, a fact no one on the crew really wants to acknowledge since the trek east is only days away.

At the moment, McT hangs freely from the side of the forty-foot set, giving the assistant directors a scare. He smiles: "You forget. I made my last movie hanging from the canopy of a rain-forest. I'm used to this stuff." McTiernan is out there to demonstrate Arnold's action: Holding onto the very same electrical cables used to shock The Ripper into submission, Slater is to rappel down the side of the building and stand on the end of a cannon-shaped waterspout. Balancing his weight between cannon and cables, he's to reach out to Danny, who dangles upside down from a gargoyle on the other side of this urban chasm. When done properly, this Herculean effort will leave him a few feet below Danny with a maddening inch or two gap still be-

tween them after they both reach out. Danny must fight every instinct in his body to hold on to the gargoyle with his legs, let go with both hands and trust that his favorite movie hero can defy real-world physics long enough to catch him and swing him to safety. McT has decided that the bricks are too slippery for Arnold to negotiate and orders realistic-looking metal reinforcements to be dressed into the set as footholds.

Meanwhile, Austin tests the harness which pulls him up eighteen feet into position beneath the eagle-shaped gargoyle. The problem is that he hasn't been able to get his legs around the gargoyle's thick base. The added weight of his wetsuit, the rain pelting down and the restricting nature of his harness have made this seemingly simple task extraordinarily difficult for the boy.

McTiernan has very few options. He must combine Austin's hanging on for dear life in the same shot with Arnold coming to the rescue or the audience simply will not believe it's happening. Austin has only managed to position his legs for a few moments—not long enough for the shots—and the effort has sapped his concentration and strength beyond the point of continuing.

Nobody is harder on Austin than he is on himself. More than once he is brought down to rest with fiery determination and frustration mixed on his young face. "He's an eleven-year-old going on twenty-eight as far as I'm concerned," says stunt coordinator Joel Kramer with admiration. "Those harnesses hurt. And with the wetsuit on there's a real danger of overheating. It was tough, no question." Austin continues to face the challenge bravely and with humor, pretending to fly each time he's taken up and laughing at the Batman symbol the electricians jokingly flash on the walls between takes with their spotlights.

A blue screen is positioned on the floor in the alley between the two buildings so that McTiernan can matte in the twenty floors that beckon our heroes downward. Since rain would interfere with this delicate effects process, it will be added to the shot afterwards and Austin can work without the wetsuit.

85

Jack Slater (Arnold Schwarzenegger) helps Danny Madigan out of a perilous situation.

(Opposite, above) Danny Madigan (Austin O'Brien) clutches desperately to a stone gargoyle, many stories high over the streets of New York.

(Opposite, below) Jack Slater finds himself cornered by The Ripper on a rooftop.

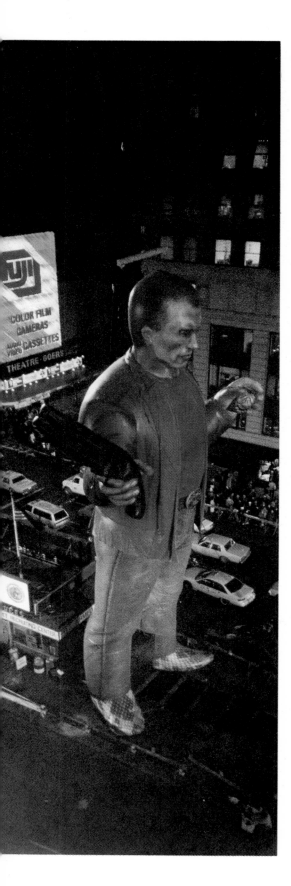

The change is just enough to make a difference. Austin gains purchase with his feet and holds there, solid. The camera rolls. Arnold makes his descent, his dialogue possessing a double meaning the writers never intended: "Hang on, Danny. Hold on, I'll be right there!" Austin does. As you look down from the rooftop at these two characters hovering over the patch of soulless blue, you can almost imagine the heartstopping abyss McTiernan plans to place beneath them.

They've got the shot. The cameras cut and Austin descends into a sea of hugs and pats on the back. McT peers down from the rooftop. "Good job, Austin!"

"Thank you, sir!" The hardest part is over for the young actor. Too bad Arnold still has to repeat his strenuous rappel a dozen times for the several angles McTiernan needs to complete the sequence. No sweat. Arnold shrugs his shoulders between takes. "What can I tell you? I need a new line of work."

THE BIG BIG APPLE...

"Arnold Schwarzenegger shut down Times Square and that's never been done before," says Carl Goldstein proudly. The weather has warmed to an unseasonal 42° F, putting everyone in a good mood on their first night shooting in the real New York. The sixty-three police officers assigned to tonight's shoot work with the production assistants to cordon off the square from the 16,000 people hoping to see Arnold. Red carpet leads into the RKO Twin theater, now dressed for the world premiere of *Jack Slater IV*. Seventh Avenue is lined with limousines waiting for their cues, and yes, Arnold's "formal" Humvee waits at the entrance, no longer a trick of fiber optic lighting. There's even a five-story balloon of Jack Slater standing over the festive proceedings.

That almost wasn't the case. While city officials never threatened to withdraw their support, a grassroots protest against the balloon almost "blew up" in the production's face...

On Monday, March 1st, the day before shooting was to begin, a team of twenty men and women descended on Times Square with fans and ropes to inflate the long flat, roughly human-shaped blob of colored plastic they had rolled out into the square. As it bobbed back and forth in the wind, gaining height, spectators tried to guess its identity. Clint Eastwood? Superman? Sam Donaldson? Guesses were favoring Schwarzenegger. Then people noticed what balloon-man held in his left hand—three sticks of balloon dynamite.

Just days earlier, the city had been devastated by a terrorist attack on the World Trade Center. No one knew yet how many lives had been lost, but New Yorkers from all walks of life considered the dynamite an exploitative joke in very poor taste, not realizing that the balloon had been in the works for months now and was a crucial storypoint in the movie.

Calls flooded in. As Bob Relyea remembers, "It's not that any-

body was being insensitive. It's just that we were so engrossed with our work, we never even thought of the connection. The Mayor's office said, 'This is kind of a sensitive area right now. A stick of dynamite that size? Please.' We said 'You couldn't be more right.'"

Several options were considered. Hide the dynamite under some kind of tarp? Matte it in later as an effect? McTiernan felt they could lose the balloon entirely, if necessary, but Zanetti, ever the production designer, was adamant that it stay. "I thought about the mythical aspect of the hero in our lives and felt that Slater deserved his own statue. He got a balloon."

While several people are given credit for the ultimate solution, only one person actually did the work. Surrounded by armed guards, a professional seamstress spent the night huddled over the deflated hero in the middle of Times Square, sewing madly. She removed the badge from his belt and sewed it onto an improvised wallet. The wallet was then sewn into the remnants of the dynamite-less hand. While she was at it, she tucked in the balloon's chin slightly, helping increase its likeness to Schwarzenegger. The world's largest "plastic surgery" was successful on both counts.

In New York City, a 75-foot-high balloon of Jack Slater stands outside a theater in Times Square for the premiere of *Jack Slater IV*.

89

PLANET HOLLYWOOD

Walking into Planet Hollywood is like walking into the movie-world of Jack Slater; props, costumes and set pieces live on here, ageless, magical decorations for the restaurant crowd. But you're not here to eat. Go through the door marked PRIVATE and you will discover a room few visitors ever see—a full-sized movie theater. It's no surprise, given the restaurant's owners, but it was certainly generous of Schwarzenegger to make it the location screening room for dailies. Bleary-eyed crew members treat themselves to coffee and food as they watch yesterday's work on the screen. The premiere footage looks beautiful. And the long telephoto shots of Danny and Slater running through the crowds towards the theater are intense. There is a chuckle when Co-producer Neal Nordlinger appears on screen as a red-coated valet tending Schwarzenegger's monster vehicle. "You know, there are a lot of similarities between producing and parking cars," he jokes. "Knowing when to change gears, dressing sharp, stuff like that."

"I don't know how anyone makes a movie in New York City," says McTiernan rolling his eyes. "There's a million people everywhere! You hire a production assistant just to stand in each parking space you need so that two days later there's a place to park the equipment. It's nuts. What's even more amazing is that New York production people take it in stride. They think it's normal to hire three hundred pa's. But I must say, the government of the

Danny Madigan (Austin O'Brien and Jack Slater (Arnold Schwarzenegger) on the streets of New York.

The premiere of *Jack Slater IV*

City of New York really extended themselves to be generous to us."

"Let's talk Forty-Second Street," says Goldstein, "which is the main artery for traffic coming from Port Authority. Tens of thousands of people pour through there every hour during rush hour and we needed to shut it down starting at 3 p.m. to shoot the scenes outside the Pandora. The cops were laughing at us. They said it'd never happen, but they managed to find a way to do it for us. I was blown away."

Crowds were ever-present, not all of them friendly. Despite warnings on all radio and TV stations, commuters were still surprised to find their daily route interrupted for a movie. One editorial cartoon had a cabdriver with miles of cars piled up behind him taking a sharp stick to the Slater balloon, shouting "Haven't you heard of jaywalking, pal?"

And as the days progressed, cold weather returned with a vengeance, making the work day seem even longer. "We had a joke before the picture started," recalls Bob Relyea. "We said, 'What if we go to New York at the end of the shooting schedule and it turns out to be the blizzard of the century?' I wasn't laughing at the end." So far, McTiernan had managed to make use of the sporadic snowfall, incorporating it into the final shot of the film, but if a major storm hit it would without doubt paralyze the production.

Dealing with these and other pressures, the crew began to look forward to dailies at Planet Hollywood, taking refuge from the madness outside and escaping into Jack Slater's world, watching scenes in New York rather than making them...

And as Brian Cook announced, "That's a wrap," on their final day in the city, the first snowflakes from the "Blizzard of the Century" hit the ground. Now, if only there was some way to get home...

In a sequence deleted from the film, Jack Slater is asked for his autograph by a group of Halloween trick-or-treaters who mistake him for Arnold Schwarzenegger.

12

DID SOMEONE SAY...ACTION?

"I kept getting involved in these crazy adventures—but the craziest thing was I kept surviving." —**Jack Slater**

"Wile E. Coyote is one my film consultants." —**John McTiernan**

"I don't think the movie would have worked if we hadn't gone beyond what had been done in the past," says Schwarzenegger. "You're zeroing in on this action hero and you have to show him doing those action movie things in a way that's bigger than anything we've seen before."

Taking the action off the written page and putting it up on the screen fell largely on the shoulders of second unit directors Fred Waugh and Vic Armstrong and stunt coordinator Joel Kramer. Whether it was car chases or fight sequences or falls from high places, their assignment was specific: Make Slater believably indestructible.

BONNEVILLE ADVENTURES

The alley between Columbia's soundstages looks like a used car lot, as vehicles of every shape and size wait for their screen tests. A movie hero's car is an important expression of his character and today the dominant motif is convertibles. Fiery red ones (too small). Baby blue ones with engines bulging under their hoods (doesn't match the costume). Even Schwarzenegger's infamous Humvee (also a convertible) is given a shot at stardom.

Soon two vehicles are left at the audition. McT has fallen in love with a 1967 Shelby Mustang Cobra. "Very restrained and tasteful," he will declare later, "but with eighteen-inch monster truck tires. I saw it as an adaptation Slater had made for his lifestyle. He liked the sports car, but he needed something that could drive up stairs once in a while so he's modified it."

Arnold prefers "the single most awesome '66 Bonneville Convertible ever abused by its action-movie owner," as the script describes it. In reality, it's a boat-sized slab of American steel with a rather somber paint job and garish red leather interior. There's nothing particularly awesome about it...until you see it move.

It's oversized body and high-powered engine make it much more suited to the stunts in the film. "The Mustang, with its shorter wheel base, couldn't get much done," explains Kramer. "especially when you're sliding into corners at certain speeds and playing chicken with other cars. The Bonneville has more weight to push." Of course that weight is going to be pushed into about every imaginable angle one can imagine—into other cars, onto two wheels, and across flood control channels.

The Mustang is rolled into deep storage.

Over the next few weeks, the transportation department procures and revamps nine perfect clones of the chosen Bonneville,

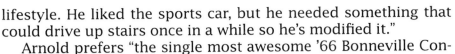

updating them with the latest brakes and suspension systems. Fuel cells replace gas tanks to eliminate the danger of fire. Nascar seatbelts are bolted onto the frames and hidden roll cages are welded around the passenger compartment. From there, different cars are modified to perform different tasks.

"Certain cars were built for jumps," elaborates Kramer. "Others for high-speed chases, others for crashes and still others just for the actors to sit in. After you crash one car you want others standing by so you don't shut down the whole production. Plus, everything's synchronized. I have to work closely with Tommy Fisher to come up with a lot of the rigs we use. There's a lot of trial and error involved."

While it sounds dangerous to experiment with two tons of steel, filmmakers are always trying to to spice up what threatens to become yet-another-LA-car-chase. In this instance, McTiernan wanted Slater to crash through the stone safety-railing of the First Street Bridge and sail to a safe landing in the cement-covered flood control channels of the LA river. Sound familiar? Arnold did it on a motorcycle in *Terminator 2* using cables that were then removed from the shot digitally.

In this instance, there is concern that a cabled descent won't look realistic, especially since the tremendous weight of the Bonneville will require more stringent safety constraints for the height involved. Instead, they decide to try an unmanned launch using a high-pressure air cannon and dummies in place of stuntmen. The completed assembly is christened the "ACME SCUD LAUNCHER" and if a car is ever to be launched into orbit, this is the rig that will make it happen. 3-2-1, KAPOW! Zero to sixty in .02 seconds! The fall is such a great distance, however, that the Bonneville still noses forward before hitting the slanted

floor of the canal eighty feet below. Both dummies are crushed as the vehicle folds in half from the force of the impact. Time for another Bonneville.

The launch, however, looks fantastic. A different rig can land the car, allowing the stunt team to use a cabled descent that is slower and safer. The results are impressive. In one day they manage to fly the car an astonishing seventeen times. Ladies and gentlemen, please do not try this at home.

Getting the car into the canal completes the T2 homage. Now the filmmakers want to top it by flying the car back out. Another special rig is built. The 900-pound fiberglass car is mounted on the end of a long crane, looking like the Dumbo ride at Disneyland. Designed to connect with a shot of the Bonneville racing up the slanted wall of the canal, the car tilts skyward on hydraulic pistons as the crane traces a parabolic arc from the lip of the canal, high into the air and onto the back of a Coca-Cola

While cannon-style launch techniques were great at sending Slater's Bonneville airborne into the LA River Basin, special wire rigs created by Tommy Fisher's special effects crew were needed to land the car safely and controllably.

ARNOLD BEHIND THE WHEEL? BIG MISTAKE!

John McTiernan's interest in how Slater drove during normal circumstances (to the supermarket as opposed to two-wheeled chases in reverse) became a running joke in the film. "It's not a question of having respect for the road. He just has no awareness of obstacles at all. He drives through them."

It's quite possible this character trait was derived from a small reputation Arnold has achieved over the years. "He's great when it comes to stopping on the mark," said Peter Kent, but that's only part of the job. On *Raw Deal* he killed two transmissions in a row by driving over the same rock twice. On *Kindergarten Cop* he

left a car in neutral. Those in the crew that weren't bent over laughing were able to catch the car as it rolled backwards down the hill! Candid moments such as these have earned Schwarzenegger a reputation as a "spirited" driver.

It was no surprise when he committed a non-moving violation during *Last Action Hero*. Danny is trying to dissuade Jack from playing chicken against Benedict shortly after their arrival in the real world. Austin O'Brien recalls, "I'm telling him that he's gonna crash and he slams on the gas and the car doesn't go anywhere!" As realization dawns, Arnold looks sheepishly straight into the camera...

"Forgot to put it in gear." At which point he speeds off, take ruined, crew in stitches.

Did protégé O'Brien pick up any driving tips from the master? If the script is any indication...

Danny hits the gas. FISHTAILS. Executes the clumsiest U-turn in screen HISTORY —

        SLATER
Do you...know how to drive..?

        DANNY
Sure, I watched you do it.

SLATER reacts in terror.

truck driving next to the canal. From there, the ACME SCUD LAUNCHER will send Slater's car flying over the front of the semi and back onto the road. Happy motorin'!

"The hardest thing about a car chase is not doing the chase itself. That I enjoy," shares Kramer. "It's connecting the pieces with what the director wants, finding the right locations and making sure each element is set up right. That's the headache."

And if, by chance, it doesn't work, crash two Bonnevilles and call your director in the morning.

Leaping Slaters!

The location is Jack Slater's ex-wife's house in the Hollywood Hills. Benedict and his thugs have just high-tailed it and Slater must give chase. Rushing out to the balcony, he sees the black sedan speeding down the winding road. Without a second thought, Slater runs to the balcony and leaps...

And the camera follows!

"We did things that have never been done before," smiles Kramer. "It's the movie-within-the-movie at this point so we can really exaggerate the action. We had Slater jump off the balcony, fly out and down ten feet to a railing, do a handstand, spring up, do a complete flip and drop sixty feet onto solid ground—all in one shot. It was a real challenge for us to put that together."

It looks like Spiderman would be more at home here than Jack Slater as cables and rigging extends out over the hillside like a high-tech web. In the middle of it, stunt-double Bob Brown is harnessed to two cables extending from either side of his waist up to a tension controller and then up and around finally connecting to Lane Leavitt's descender rig.

Vic Armstrong brings a twist to the set-up by incorporating the camera move into the jump. "All the rigging was in place, why not add a second descender for a man carrying a stripped-down camera?" Now the audience's heart will pound with Slater's as they follow the hero into open space...

Will The Real Jack Slater...

Brown was one of five stuntmen to double Schwarzenegger. Kramer did a lot of the vehicle stunts himself. But on the frequent occasions that a more convincing-looking Schwarzenegger double was called for, the assignment fell to actor and stunt-double Peter Kent, who has doubled for Arnold since *Terminator*. Wearing a prosthetic make-up designed especially for his face by Jeff Dawn, Kent can pass for Schwarzenegger from almost every angle except dead on. The only give-away is that he's three inches taller than Arnold and can't move his lips in the makeup. While Kent enjoys dodging bullets, causing explosions, hanging from glass elevators and falling seventy feet into artificial tar, the make-up gets to him after a while. At the end of the day he relishes ripping off the foam latex and letting his skin breath, often making newcomers a bit squeamish. "I cannot stress how important it is to use a really good sunblock," he smiles, peeling off a chunk of his left cheek. "With the ozone the way it is, you can never be too careful these days." [Kent's real face can be seen at the *Jack Slater IV* premiere, as the man who refuses to let The Ripper in without a tuxedo.]

GOODBYE, LEO

By far, the rooftop funeral for mafioso Leo the Fart epitomizes the achievements of Kramer and crew. Beginning in an alley with a string of "I got you's" and "No, I got you's" and ending in an avalanche of gunfire, a plummeting elevator, an out-of-control helicopter, a 360-foot crane, and a twenty story freefall into the La Brea Tarpits, the sequence is a tour de force of imagination and excitement.

"My God, this man is NOT DEAD!" cries Slater in a thinly veiled attempt to steal Leo's four-hundred-pound corpse from under the noses of three hundred armed men in reverent attendance. He has four minutes to get the nerve gas–carrying body to minimum safe distance before Leo can pass gas one last time! "THIS MAN NEEDS A DOCTOR!" he shouts, hoisting the quarter-ton body from it's piano-sized coffin and hoofing it to the edge of the roof. Danny's crane hook approaches...and keeps on going... stranding our hero in a most unusual pickle. He's gonna have to punch his way out.

"It's like all of my careers are converging for this scene," Arnold laughs. The Leo dummy has been built to possess real weight, giving Arnold a major workout with each take. "The bodybuilding lets me run with this much weight and the acting helps show my amazed shock when the crane misses me. I love this stuff."

"I'd say Arnold did almost eighty percent of the stunts in that sequence," says Joel. "You can't ask for a better fight man. He's a real thinker. Never misses a beat. We choreographed stuff where Slater's running down the waterfall being shot at and ducking in the elevator to let the helicopter gunship take out all these guys in the lobby. Every move, every punch, every bit of timing— Arnold doesn't miss anything."

"It's a great pleasure when I can do my own stunts. I enjoy the physical stuff. The trick is knowing how far to go. At what point do you want someone else with special training to double you? I leave those judgments to Joel Kramer, whom I trust very much. Generally, his rule is that if I can get killed then he'll let someone else do it That's the usual rule about those things!" laughs Arnold.

It is Peter Kent's turn to double for Arnold in the special elevator rig built by Tommy Fisher. "The elevator is supposed to look like it's tearing off the building, but it's actually hinged," explains Kent. "The problem is that you're not really sure. What

Jack Slater (Arnold Schwarzenegger) clings to a crane while perched on the corpse of Leo the Fart.

if the hinges fail? You're up there twenty stories, basically getting spit out of the elevator, and you've got one full second there where you're just waiting to get caught by your cables. It's intense."

"I want a safety factor of at least fifteen to one," says Kramer. "If a man weighs two hundred pounds, I want a cable that's going to hold eight thousand pounds, and then I use two of them. It's a mental thing. If a stuntman knows that the one cable can pick up a car, with two there's no way anything can go wrong. He performs better."

Cabling such as this allows Kent and Schwarzenegger both to take turns dangling from the legs of Leo the Fart who gets caught on Danny's hook. A radio is buried in the dummy's leg, allowing ground crew to give direction as the actor and stuntman fly three hundred feet overhead. Of the stunt, Schwarzenegger later comments, "Definitely an E-ticket, that one."

The scene is set. Jack Slater drops from a 300-foot crane, scrambling in mid-air to avoid the detonating body of Leo the Fart. He plummets, the laws of gravity taking their toll until—SHGLALOOP! He is swallowed by the La Brea Tarpits. Animatronic dinosaurs stare passively at the oozing tower of goo, only recognizable as Schwarzenegger by the whites of his eyes and his super-white smile. He motions to the Tyranosaurus: "See? In this movie we have the *Last Action Hero* and *Jurassic Park!*"

In the next shot, Slater is all but perfectly clean. Danny is suspicious. "You know, tar actually sticks to some people,"

This isn't tar. A safer substitute has been found. "It's the stuff they make the cookie part of Oreos with," elucidated stunt-double Peter Kent. "Hideous stuff. You need that skin barrier cream mechanics use, otherwise you come out all brown-green. This is edible?"

Schwarzenegger is in full agreement. "There is nothing chocolate about it. It totally tastes like this weird fungus kind of thing." Of course, that may be an effect of having stood in the rain and sun for several weeks.

Though the disgust of both men is obvious, for once it is Arnold who bears the brunt of the dirty job. "I just fall in and get out again," says Kent. "But Arnold has to duck under and

surface and really swim around in there. He's slathered up with that stuff."

At the end of the day, Arnold looks more like the creature from the Black Lagoon than an action hero. His hair has become a black shiny helmet, packed in the greasy substance. On *Predator*, McTiernan kept Schwarzenegger packed in oily mud for weeks. "It's the only time I've seen him get cranky," the director recalls. Thankfully for Schwarzenegger and Kent, today is a one-time thing.

"I'll never eat another Oreo cookie as long as I live," vows Kent.

THE "COYOTE MOMENT"

Convincing audiences of Jack Slater's indestructibility was not always the sole responsibility of the stuntmen. Close coordination with visual effects staff was often necessary. After all, unlike circus performers who work with safety nets in full view, filmmakers can remove their nets after the fact, making everything seem much more dangerous than it really is.

The metal brace snaps and Slater plummets from the broken glass elevator, heading for pavement twenty stories below. You can almost read the words once again etched in his weary features as he falls, like the double-blink of a cartoon character before physics catches up to the fact that he's just walked off a cliff.

"McTiernan is extremely fond of the Wile E. Coyote cartoons," explains Neal Nordlinger. "He's shot into outerspace, he's run over by trucks, but he always gets up and tries again, no matter how disgruntled he is. And that's the kind of tone he wanted Slater to have in movie-world."

Creating an incredible high fall was not new for McTiernan. He had dealt with a similar problem on *Die Hard*, sending Alan Rickman falling thirty-six feet into a blue screen covered airbag. What he wants to try this time is to follow the actor as he falls, to really capture his expression on the way down. This requires sending a heavy camera rig down right on top of him. "It's a dangerous scenario," comments visual effects supervisor John Sullivan. "We used two separate cable rigs to have the camera follow him at a slightly slower rate. This allowed us to stay close to his face, and still capture some of the freefall effect McT wanted."

When the descender spools are triggered, Arnold and the camera rig drop a preset fifty feet. Shot at ten times normal speed, the fall is stretched from two seconds into twenty. At the last possible second, the spools activate their brakes, leaving actor and camera dangling above the blue screen covered stuntpads.

Results are disappointing. Several reasons are cited. "If we were dropped like that, our faces would vibrate in the intense wind," explains Neal Nordlinger. "But Arnold has no body fat. You can't tell that he's falling." It is also obvious that the rig is physically restricting—Arnold's arms keep running into his cables. And lastly, the fall is too fast. There's no time to react. By the time Arnold has started his "Wile E. Coyote moment" the breaks have started to decelerate.

Perhaps additional height is the solution. A new rig is built and Arnold is asked to try again. "John McTiernan is trying for the non-compromise picture and Arnold understands that," says Bob Relyea. "He wears

the two hats of actor and executive producer quite successfully: If you go to him as an actor and say, 'Listen, I know you haven't had much rest but we're going to hook you up to some wires again and drop you seventy feet,' he'll slip on the hat of the executive producer and say, 'Okay,' because he understands production problems and the director's need for getting that shot."

This time the results are about the same, stilted and unspectacular. The reaction just isn't happening the way McTiernan envisions it. The double descender approach is scrapped.

Then Vic Armstrong suggests a new approach. Since it's blue screen anyway, why is Arnold traveling downwards? Why not travel sideways? Instead of a descender rig, why not a trapeze? Arnold is game to try anything, knowing that if it works it can only help the picture. Suspended from a two-hundred-foot crane arm, he's let go, gently falling away from camera with about three times the amount of time to create the performance McT is trying so hard to capture.

The results are incredibly successful. McTiernan is pleased. Months of trial and error have finally paid off in the final days of production. Now, it's up to Neil Krepela at Boss Film to remove all traces of the stunt rigging. "I think McTiernan really used the technology and machinery to create a great character moment," says Krepela. "After all this stuff has happened to Slater, that one piece of metal breaking is the last straw. And seeing that look on Arnold's face as he falls is priceless."

Wires removed, the audience will never miss what they never saw. They'll only see our hero flash a coyote-like "Why me?" to the heavens as he plummets twenty stories to his death.

Well…maybe not. After all, this is Jack Slater. He'll think of something.

No Cuts

If cartoon-like exaggeration was the key to the stuntwork in movie-world, understatement was the key in real-world New York. As McTiernan recalls, "I just saw the car crash we staged in the alley. There are no cuts in it. You really see Arnold drive off in a car and collide head on with a New York taxicab at about forty miles an hour. Totally smashes up. And for like thirty seconds afterwards nothing happens. There's a lot of smoke, but there's dead silence. Arnold doesn't get out. And we actually follow Austin as he runs two hundred yards down the alley and up to the smashed cars. And it's like…'I can't believe it.' This was important. I wanted the audience to have the feeling they were really there. We've spent a great deal of effort to actually do things as opposed to mocking them up or creating an effect."

"It was a great challenge for everyone doing stunts in both worlds," adds Schwarzenegger, "for the most part these are entirely new stunts we've created for this movie and that always brings a lot of excitement to the screen."

(Opposite) A massive trapeze-style rig was assembled for Arnold to cheat his fall in a new direction. While still requiring body harnesses and cables, the actor could now perform somersaults and backflips worthy of Superman. Said Schwarzenegger, "It really is like flying."

Jack Slater and the tough Asian play a little game of "Chicken" in the real world.

13

THROUGH THE LOOKING GLASS WITH JOHN McTIERNAN

He's considered one of the best directors in the action genre, but you would not guess it from his peaceful assured demeanor. He's a man who spends much of his time in his mind, wrestling with the creative and technical problems at hand. When he speaks it tends to be terse. When he expresses joy it tends to be childlike, but brief. And when he creates...look out. This man made Arnold Schwarzenegger run for his life in *Predator*. He transformed a building into a battlezone in *Die Hard*. He made the cold war even colder in *The Hunt for Red October*. And he portrayed the battle of one culture against another in *Medicine Man*. Because each project has been based firmly on content rather than form, he's managed to avoid the clichés of his chosen field. As the assistant directors were quick to point out at the beginning of the production, "Top man in his field and he's never done a car chase. Incredible." Now, John McTiernan is confronting those clichés head on, in a film about movies, life and that magical area somewhere in between.

Q: How did your involvement with the project change the script?

A: There was invention in the script that stood out. It had a wicked sense of humor, which, I guess, I softened some. You get a sense that these people, our two protagonists are kind of nice. The original had a good deal more...meanness in it, for lack of a better word. It was funny, to be sure, but it was also a great deal more violent. That's probably something that Arnold and I changed. To some extent, the production executives thought they were just buying *Lethal Weapon* with Arnold in it. Then Arnold and I changed it, because it isn't *Lethal Weapon* with Arnold.

Q: Why do you feel the action genre was ripe for parody?

A: The great thing about attacking a genre is you can use the audience's knowledge of the tired formula as a kind of "theatri-

cal jujitsu," employing what they think is going to happen as the momentum to throw them. It's fun. But I'd say the movie is more of a comedy adventure which uses action movies as a springboard. Both characters get transported through the looking glass in one way or another. Also, its a coming of age story for Danny, in the tradition of *Treasure Island* or *Kidnapped* by Robert Louis Stevenson, which makes it a little warmer, hopefully, than what's at the heart of most action pictures.

Q: The movie also has fun with a lot of Arnold's career. Why do you think Arnold decided this was the right time for him to have a little fun with his fame?

A: I shouldn't speak for Arnold, but after you've made *Terminator 2* where are you going to go, except backwards if you're trying to do the same thing again? Arnold and Cameron really knocked it. The genre's dead for a while. No prudent person will try and top it for several years. So, what's next? His ability to laugh at himself has always been at the heart of his charm, so to play with that using his sense of wit and his self-effacing nature fit right in with the tone of this script.

Director John McTiernan (right) and Arnold Schwarzenegger chat between takes while shooting on the top of the Empire State Building in New York City.

Director John McTiernan (right) consults with cinematographer Dean Semler on location in New York City.

Q: As the director, how did you create the two worlds that the audience experiences in the movie?

A: I think the two worlds have an influence on each other, so it isn't as extreme as you might think. Our experience of the action-packed movie-world changes once Danny is in it because we share his perceptions. And when Slater enters our world, all of a sudden it isn't all long lenses and quick cuts and things. It takes him a while to get used to it though Danny does his best to explain it to him.

Q: You've shot movies under incredibly difficult circumstances. In jungles, in submarines. Now, you were faced with shooting in Manhattan. Times Square and Forty-Second Street.

A: The jungle.

Q: At one point there was some talk about not shooting in New York and maybe trying to fake it?

A: The conceit of this film is that you're coming out of the movie screen and into the real world. And you've said that it's New York, so it better look like New York. You can fake up New York in any number of ways, but all of them would be pretty

inappropriate for this particular script. In fact, it would look outright foolish, as if you hadn't bothered to read it.

Q: Why is Danny so enthralled by Jack Slater movies?

A: The obvious answer is that Jack's a male role model in Danny's life. The less obvious answer is that Jack is an effective person in a world that leaves most people powerless. That's another reason why the story had to take place in New York City, where it's nearly impossible to do anything. Danny feels impotent in the literal sense of the word, totally at the mercy of this Orwellian *1984* world. So he fantasizes about Jack Slater, this person who isn't stopped by obstacles. That may be my own preoccupation more than the script's. I went to New York for the first time when I went to college. I'd grown up in a fairly small place and it was like going to another world; certainly like going to another country. I just felt devastated for years. I mean, I still hate the place [chuckles]. I sort of break into a cold sweat when I hit the airport. For exactly this reason; there's so many people and its so difficult to do anything.

Q: How does Slater's trip to the real world change him?

A: This is something Bill Goldman brought to the script and something I had trouble communicating to some of the earlier writers. My philosophy was that the story can only be about

Slater going beyond what was scripted for him. It can only be about the fact that Pinocchio has some of the makings of a real boy; that the cardboard movie hero is capable of some observations and actions that weren't there in the script, that he has feelings and emotions beyond what the studio executives thought would sell. There's just a tiny spark inside him that could become a real person. And once that spark, that potential, happens to stumble into this little kid from the real world it starts to blossom.

Q: What does Danny learn from Jack?

A: He learns to be brave and Jack learns to be vulnerable. Isn't that how the dialogue goes? [smiles] The story works much better from the Slater perspective than it does from the boy's because Slater's change is so clear cut. With Danny there's a whole collection of things in the realm of learning to live in the real world, learning to face his responsibilities. Simply put, the boy learns some confidence and fights some of the demons in his own life because of his exposure to the hero.

On another level, Danny learns that fantasies have their limitations. They certainly aren't any better and maybe they aren't as good as real life. It's harder to talk about because it's more subtle. As New York spreads everywhere else, as everything becomes more crowded and it becomes more difficult to do anything, there will be more and more synthetic experiences. There are already major corporations who say that their business is manufacturing and marketing synthetic experiences. Eisner said

(Opposite) (left to right) Director John McTiernan, cinematographer Dean Semler (standing center, behind camera) and Arnold Schwarzenegger.

(Below) Cinematographer Dean Semler, John McTiernan (sitting) and Arnold Schwarzenegger on the Los Angeles police station set.

it about Disney. It's certainly what this corporation does. For example, we collectively spend billions of dollars going to Egypt to re-create the experience of some nineteenth-century explorer who went there when it was an uncharted place and dug all these ruins out of the sand and we end up on a bus with thousands of other folks. But through a movie, your experience can be much closer to the nineteenth-century explorer's than would ever be possible sitting on the bus. Who's to say which experience is more real? The celluloid recreation or the tourist bureau's?

Q: There has been discussion about the fact that this movie is being geared to a PG-13 release instead of an R. Is there a message you hope this film will communicate to younger audiences?

A: I don't believe in explicit messages. I don't think they ever actually accomplish what their nominal purpose is. I do believe in implicit ones. You send messages far more clearly by doing rather than saying. This is a movie. I put less violence in this movie. I don't have to make a campaign about the fact that I'm doing it. I'm just doing it. In one version of the script Danny solved the conflict at the end with a gun he'd brought with him out of the movie. I made sure that version didn't happen. You just can't bloody do it. You can't go out and say, "Okay kids, the real solution is to get yourself a gun! It'll solve all your problems!" The movie isn't an anti-violence campaign by any means, but I think implicitly the movie clearly shows how Danny's reaction to real-world violence is delineated from his taste for cinematic violence. And as I said before, this is a gentler movie now than it was.

Q: When you were young, what were some of your favorite movies? And, if you had Danny's magic ticket, what movies would you like to visit?

A: *Ben Hur. King Kong* was an incredible jouney of the imagination as well. The problem with the magic ticket fantasy is that the films I liked as a boy are not films I'd want to visit now. "You want to go to *Spartacus*?" Hell, no! You see what happened to those guys at the end?! Or *Gorgo*. Remember that one? I'd like to visit any number of John Ford westerns, like *The Horse Soldiers* or *My Darling Clementine*. The feeling in that film makes it a world I'd like to visit.

Q: All of your projects have contained a certain amount of humor, but this is by far the most broad. How has has it been to play with the comedic aspects of this movie?

A: I take a certain perverse joy in doing things that people find amusing, especially since everyone seems to think that I'm so somber and serious. If you really look at *Die Hard* it was filled with these [snaps fingers] jokes. So was *Hunt for Red October*. With action stuff you've got to shoot it in these two to five second dribs and drabs because it's mostly achieved in the editing. You create all the pieces and then put them together in such a way that they look like one real event. Most comedy, by contrast, depends on the actors and the timing of their interaction, so you tend to work in more sustained pieces. We've just finished cutting the scene where Slater is stealing the body at the rooftop funeral scene. It's hysterical. And Arnold is so good at it that it's amazing. He may end up as Governor or something, but if he wants to I really think he could do a Cary Grant kind of film, soon. He's got this gentle, straightforward charm that he can project on screen. Several generations of movie stars made their living on that simple ability. It's nowhere near as simple as you think.

There's a great deal of comedy built into the action, too, I should add. I have this theory that all we're trying to do is recreate Saturday morning cartoons for ourselves as adults. I think the difference between European cinema and American films is that they didn't have Wile E. Coyote.

14

POLISHING UP REALITY

DANNY
You say this is a real police station?
An animated cat just walked in.

SLATER
And he'll do it again tomorrow,
what's your point?

From the start it was clear that the unusual combination of fantasy and reality that defines Jack Slater's movie-world would call upon almost every kind of visual effect developed to date. It was also clear that many of the effects would only be successful to the extent that they "hid" reality, removing stunt cables or other special rigs that would otherwise reveal the secrets of Slater's indestructibility. "This movie is based on our shared experience of what it's like inside the world of movies," explains co-producer Neal Norlinger. "We extend reality, polish it up a bit. It's an exaggerated place where real people can do impossible things." With this in mind, it was decided early on that the effects didn't have to be groundbreaking. They merely had to be the best. And that meant taking advantage of the digital realm.

DIGITAL DREAMS

Consider this. The first movie camera was made from the guts of a sewing machine. The film itself was little more than a strip of nitrate coated with a chemical goo which reacted to patterns of shadow and light. As crude as this process seems today, magicians of the day recognized it for what it was—a new magic had arrived. Their days of smoke and mirrors were numbered. But no matter how hard generations of visionaries worked to improve the technology, their cinematic illusions were always compromised somehow, chained to the limitations of the chemical goo.

IN EVERY FRAME

"I don't really like you, all right? You've brought me nothing but pain."
—Jack Slater to Arnold Schwarzenegger

"Twinning" is an old standard of the visual effects repertoire, improved in recent years by sophisticated motion control equipment, and now the technique has been freed completely of its photochemical limitations. Digital effects artist Jacques Stroweis has made each of the four hundred or so frames (about sixteen seconds) perfect. So when Slater meets his real world counterpart for the first time, there will be no telltale matte lines. The murkiness and specks of dirt that often creep into complex optical effects will be nonexistent.

But this is not what makes the shot remarkable. Now that Arnold's two performances have been married together in the same frame, one thing becomes immediately clear. Arnold Schwarzenegger is one heck of an actor.

Maybe Shakespeare isn't his strong point, but compare the

two faces: Arnold playing Arnold is a brilliant caricature of himself: a huckster, a wheeler dealer, no more substantial or trustworthy than any one of a hundred Hollywood power brokers you care to name. Arnold playing Slater, on the other hand, is a haunted man, the existential dilemma of being fictional etched into the lines of his face. The mogul taunts the hero and offers him quick money as a two-bit look-alike. Big mistake. The hero sums up Schwarzenegger for what he is and dismisses him. He's got more important things to do, like saving the world. The contrast could not be any greater. And the power of Arnold's performance(s) is apparent in every frame....

"If you compare filmmaking to music history, everything up to this point can be considered pre-Bach," explains Richard Greenberg, Visual Effects Creative Director for *Last Action Hero* and head of R/Greenberg Associates, Los Angeles division. "Because of the vast quantities of information computers can now store and manipulate, we're almost at a point where you can compose a movie in real time the way you compose music. It's a phenomenal idea."

The challenge with traditional effects work is controlling "the goo." We've all seen the electric haircut phenomenon of an actor matted into a shot poorly via blue screen. His hair shimmers because the photochemical film emulsion (or grain) could not decide where blue screen stopped and hair began, a decision made over and over again (twenty-four times each second) with constant variations due to minute changes in the grain. While you can minimize such problems, you cannot get rid of them entirely; an attempt to adjust one piece of offending emulsion disturbs the balance of hundreds of neighbors. Without the strictest quality control matte lines, color shifts, and general murkiness (from the many generations of film required to assemble each shot)

116

sneak into all but the best of shots. The audience may not know what's wrong with the image, but they can sense the manipulation.

The advantage of digital image processing is that you can manipulate an image beyond the chaos of its grain. Scanned into the computer at the highest possible level of resolution, grain is replaced by a sea of 1s and 0s that can be altered with ease, and accuracy (one grain at a time, if necessary), leaving no trace of the manipulation. And since all changes occur inside the computer, the process is generationless. The finished shot is as pristine and clear as the original negative.

And, it's relatively easy. "You mention digital image processing to someone and they think it's mathematics and complex modeling and programming. It doesn't have to be. The great thing about digital is that it can mimic tools like pencils and brushes that artists have used for thousands of years while giving them powerful new capabilities," explains Stuart Robertson, digital effects supervisor for R/Greenberg Associates, Los Angeles. "The real revolution is that the technology uses its power to become invisible, allowing the director to forget about the mechanics and to focus on creating." Once cumbersome and slow, the computer has finally achieved an agility and finesse worthy of a professional dancer, making it a perfect companion for the composers of images.

"USUALLY WHEN I DO THAT, IT LEAVES A HOLE"

"McTiernan did not want this to become an effects driven show," explains John Sullivan, visual effects supervisor for the production. "There was discussion about what Danny's pass-through into movie-world should look like and he decided the pass-through should be fast—practically instantaneous—because it's not about how Danny gets there, it's about how he reacts once he's there."

Other "pass-throughs" would be slower, allowing the filmmakers to convey the magic controlled by the ticket. "I thought it might have the same qualities as Kirlian photography," remembers Richard Greenberg, referring to the technique of sending high voltage through an object and photographing its luminous "aura." The resulting image resembles a miniature lightning storm, delicate and fractal-looking, emanating in all directions from the dark silhouette of the object.

Benedict is about to test the ticket's powers by putting his fingers through the wall. On set, the wall is replaced with a stretched rubbery membrane painted the same color. A slit is made for actor Charles Dance to reach through, while strong lights are positioned on the other side. When his fingers poke through the membrane, shafts of light stream past his hand. Then the solid wall is put back and shot from the exact same angle. The selected take is then scanned into the computer, sep-

Danny Madigan (Austin O'Brien) tests the power of his magic ticket.

arated into "channels," of red, green, blue, and luminance (brightness) information for maximum control of the available spectrum. (Digital's palette contains more than 68 billion colors.)

At RGA/LA, digital effects artist January Nordman makes it look like Benedict's fingers disappear into the wall by hiding the slit. On her screen, she uses a brush to wash away that part of the frame, revealing the solid wall footage waiting beneath. The Kirlian effect will be generated later with specially written software referenced perfectly to Nordman's alterations.

"In the finished effect Benedict's fingers create a beautiful Kirlian 'ripple' at the point they disappear," explains Robertson. "The light streaming past his hand is supposed to be the light of the projector. It's kind of cute."

PLAYING GOD WITH DEATH

Hitchcock once said that he admired Walt Disney because he had the power to tear up an actor if he didn't like the performance. In this instance, McTiernan has decided to replace Death from Bergman's *The Seventh Seal* with his own casting choice, Sir Ian McKellan. The decision is practical as much as it is aesthetic John can direct Sir Ian; the two-dimensional Death can only play chess. On set, shooting Sir Ian in front of a blue screen, McT is temporarily overwhelmed by the levels involved in the shot. "Jeez! This is special effects within special effects within special effects!" First, you have the original shot: Looking over the shoulder of death as Max Von Sydow contemplates the

118

chessboard. Then you insert Sir Ian, who is larger than the actor he's replacing and therefore functions like a "living matte." This combined image is then mapped onto the movie screen in the theater where Mercedes Ruehl is watching. And last, you have Sir Ian's scythe raking the screen, it's tip now three dimensional, Kirlian energy skittering in its wake. McTiernan has reason to be overwhelmed. Using optical techniques, this shot could have been a nightmare. Now the only nightmare is on the screen.

HERE'S LOOKING AT YOU, KID

Danny stares on as the Watch Commander pairs up partners for some of the weirdest buddy-cop movies we'll never see. "It's like every cop you've ever seen in a movie goes through this wild station," Schwarzenegger explains to actress Sharon Stone who has shown up to do her cameo. "We don't follow their stories because this is Slater's movie, but they're there. I don't think anything of it, but Danny's amazed by all of them, of course."

Including a gray-looking man in an old-fashioned trenchcoat. The Watch commander shouts, "Wohlschleager! You're partnered up with the black-and-white digitization of Humphrey Bogart as Sam Spade!" The gray man turns around. It is, indeed, Bogey.

"That was an homage to the effect we developed for the Coca-Cola spots some while ago," explains Richard Greenberg with pride. "It's amazing when you think about it. These icons from cinema's past are becoming part of our visual vocabulary. If you'd suggested that idea even ten years ago you would have been told it could never happen."

On set, John Sullivan compares two images. One is the Bogart clip, the other is the Watch Commander's desk as policemen stroll back and forth waiting for their assignments. Sullivan must match his camera work to that of a cameraman shooting decades ago. Plus he must make sure the extras don't violate Bogey's intended space, otherwise digital effects artist Laurel Klick will have problems transporting the black-and-white detective into our colorful world. Director of Photography Dean Semler has done his part for the shot by making sure

Death (Sir Ian McKellan) steps off the screen of *The Seventh Seal* to terrorize people on the streets of New York City.

his lights cast shadows in the same direction as the lights which shined on Bogart way back when.

The only one who doesn't have anything to do is the director. After all, how could McTiernan presume to direct Bogart? How could he dare to second-guess a performance that hasn't changed in forty years?

"John had fun with that one," admits Sullivan. "At the end of the shot, Bogart looks off to his left, distracted by a sound or something. And John knew exactly how to use it to sell the shot. In the movie, Slater has just been fired and this wave of shock passes through the whole squad room. John used that group reaction to motivate Bogart's head turn. So John McTiernan got to direct Bogart!"

The director smiles. "Cut! We got that." The assistant directors declare lunch. Bogart relaxes. He knows he's more than a little rusty with this sort of stuff. especially the color business. "How was I?" he asks McTiernan, looking for an honest answer, "Not too scratchy for you? Contrast okay?" The director says yes, he was great, and thanks for taking the time to come in. By the way, he loved the performance with Audrey Hepburn in *Sabrina*. Bogey says thanks and wanders outside to the trailers.

He's in luck. Arnold is outside putting another coat of vanity wax on his Humvee. Now's his chance. He approaches in his best Sam Spade swagger and suavely pulls his detective's notebook from the trenchcoat's inner pocket. "Mr. Schwarzenegger? Could I have your autograph?" Arnold is more than generous. He even poses for a couple of snapshots. Then Bogart realizes that the events of the last few minutes have been utterly impossible and swiftly vanishes in a puff of logic. As Richard Greenberg points out, "Nothing is impossible. Barring the cost of technology and time, nothing is impossible."

A BEAUTIFUL FRIENDSHIP

At Sony Pictures Imageworks' the computers have familiar names: Groucho. Audrey Hepburn. Clint Eastwood. "We've got a real powerful workstation coming soon that we're going to name Arnold," smiles Tim McGovern, Vice President and visual effects supervisor for SPI's work on the movie. "And our film recorder is Claude Rains, served by Bogart, of course." It's a very inside joke. The film recorder is the machine that translates digitally altered frames back to film. This digital/film relationship harkens back to the end of *Casablanca* when Bogart puts his arm around Rains and says, "Luis, I think this is the beginning of a beautiful friendship." A concise metaphor for the marriage of computer and film technology.

THE REAL REAL THING

"We had something as mundane as a 7-Up removal," laughs Tim McGovern of Sony Picture Imageworks. "The movie made a product placement deal with Coca-Cola, and when Danny went to the candy counter in the Pandora there was a 7-Up dispenser in the background." 7-Up is a competing product with Coke's Sprite, so Columbia decided to take advantage of digital image processing and remove the oversight. Now when Danny walks up to the candy counter, there's no logo at all.

Holy Un-Cola, Batman! Using computers to take products out is one thing. Audiences only have to worry when advertising executives realize they can put products in!

"I'll be back...but first, a word from our sponsors."

PAUL NEWMAN BLUE

Arnold sits at a grave, Yorrick's skull in hand, contemplating the universe in moody black and white.

A sound. He looks up. Guards sneak up behind him.

Wait a minute. His eyes are blue...very blue...Paul Newman blue. And his skin has that all-but-forgotten luster of golden technicolor. The rest of the image remains as before, black, colorless.

SPI was responsible for colorizing the black-and-white scenes of Danny's imagined *Hamlet*. "Nobody really knew how far to take it at first," recalls McGovern. "but if you add only a little color it looks dirty. You really have to saturate it to give it that comic book mentality."

"McTiernan wanted to show how Danny really enjoys a film and makes it more dramatic in his mind," comments John Sullivan. "By injecting Slater into *Hamlet*, he brings some of that character's flashiness and comic book color with him." Interestingly, this technique goes all the way back to the silent era when

Is Arnold contemplating his mortality or his skin color? Shot in black and white, the filmmakers decided to accentuate the material by colorizing specific elements in each shot. For the brief graveyard scene (Act V, i.), Schwarzenegger received a technicolor treatment of flesh tones and eye color.

The Ripper (Tom Noonan) and his weapon of choice, thrown with deadly accuracy, thanks to some help from the digital-effects artisans at Sony Pictures Imageworks.

black-and-white two-reelers were given an added dimension when certain parts of the film were colorized by hand! Explosions were given an orangish hue. Women's dresses were lively studies in lavender and yellow.

In Danny's *Hamlet*, exciting elements appear in color. Fire. Muzzle flashes from Hamlet's different guns. The bright red saddle blanket of Hamlet's steed. "Claudius going through the stained-glass window was tricky. Not only did we remove the wire that pulls him through, we had to colorize all the shards of glass and track them as they fell. It came together nicely."

A Near Miss

The Ripper slings his ax! It whizzes through the air, splitting atoms on its razor sharp blade! Slater ducks, falls to the left, the ax just missing a rendezvous with his face!

"I think the general public is not going to realize that that shot is not possible," smiles McGovern. "They won't realize that you'd never risk Arnold Schwarzenegger with a sharp and heavy ax that way or that you'd risk breaking a camera because it goes right into the lens. I mean, how on earth could they get all the timing down perfect in one take?"

The shot is actually composed of three separate elements. On the rooftop of the elementary school, Tom Noonan raised the ax all the way behind his back. He dropped it there, so that when he brought his arm forward to throw, his hand was empty. John Sullivan then created a motion control shot of the ax spinning forward toward the lens. Arnold was then shot against a blue screen dodging the blow. Ron Brinkman of SPI now works to combine the elements believably into the same frame, removing all of the little "unrealities." He wraps Noonan's fingers back around the handle of the ax. He adds the shadow of the ax crossing Schwarzenegger's face. He adjusts the colors and contrasts to make sure all the elements look like it was in the same place at the same time. He does everything except add sound effects for the ax!

"The first pass we made on it, McTiernan actually thought Arnold was too close to the ax. They thought that it looked too artificial," shares McGovern. "How near is a near miss, anyway? So we recomposited the shot with Arnold slightly lower and he accepted it."

Real enough to be dangerous.

Not so real as to be impossible.

Chaos

"Digital compositing is absolutely gorgeous but it's not the right approach for every shot. You have to decide when digital works against you," explains Nordlinger. Given the expensive nature of digital, filmmakers must balance creativity with commerce.

Effects company Fantasy II, under the leadership of Gene Warren, create chaos the old-fashioned way. The dynamite chase received a welcome adrenaline boost when Fantasy II rolled a large scale miniature of the ominous black minivan. Working in miniature allowed the action to be much more dynamic and destructive than would have been prudent with a stuntman in the car. Small controllable fireballs augmented several of the shots in the film, most notably the destruction of Slater's ex-wife's house, which happens in a long shot as a kind of comic exclamation point. (Poof!) Elsinore Castle's demise was a combination of computer modeling and Fantasy II brand fiery destruction.

Magic

But even in instances where digital can be used effectively, it isn't always necessary. In the case of Peter Kuran and Kevin O'Neil of Visual Concepts Engineering it's a matter of style.

"They're using every digital trick in the book current to *Terminator 2* and beyond, but the key to the whole film, this magic ticket, is for the most part being created through traditional photochemical and optical effects," observes O'Neil, "It makes a lot of sense artistically, I think. The ticket is this ancient ornate gold leaf object from the last century when film was considered more of a parlour trick than an artform or technology. We wanted our work to add to that sense of history."

Once again, the Kirlian effect became a basis for the ticket's magic, connecting it visually to the "pass-throughs" generated by RGA/LA. It was Kevin Kruchever's task to animate the thousands of tiny sparks of electricity...by hand. "There are not many people who can do this kind of electricity," O'Neil observes, "Kevin gives it a character and a personality that is unique and somewhat mischievous." (Imagine programming a computer to create mischievous lighting.) "Since it's the passport between two realities we want it totally connected to the physicality of whomever holds it. We want it to have an active quality. Otherwise, it's just a piece of paper."

No Limits

In 1926, Buster Keaton astounded audiences by walking down the aisle, over the orchestra pit and into the movie screen where he became an active participant in the story of a famous detective. The movie was called *Sherlock Jr.* and is still considered a masterpiece today. Using nothing beyond physical stage illusions and in-camera effects, Keaton careened off of mountains and through snow and off of cars, falling and flying over the different images as they popped on the screen, delighting young and old alike. Sixty-seven years later, Danny Madigan has broken that same "screen-barrier" to discover a world much more sophisticated, fantastic and frightening than anything envisioned in Keaton's time.

The cinematic natives are getting restless...

"Theoretically, visual effects are now at a point where the only obstacle is imagination," says Richard Greenberg. "I think the next ten years will be a phenomenal period of growth in terms synthesized images combined with real images, so that you don't know where one leaves off and the other begins. Why not walk into a movie? The possibilities are practically endless. They're just waiting there for someone to imagine them."

Jack Slater (Arnold Schwarzenegger) and Danny Madigan (Austin O'Brien) emerge from the movie into the real world.

FADE OUT

Saturday, April 3rd:

Arnold Schwarzenegger is hosting the largest wrap party in the history of Columbia Pictures. As one studio executive quips, "I can remember parties like this...we called them premieres." But unlike a premiere, which is staged solely for the Hollywood elite and their ever-present publicity troops, this bash is dedicated to the dedicated—the film's crew. Over a thousand artists, craftspeople and technicians crowd into stage 30, a vast and empty workspace which has been decorated for the occasion with an eclectic assortment of crashed cars, medieval furniture, inflatable Arnold balloons and other props, all veterans of the half-year production. The rest have either been blown up, shot up, torn up or shipped off to Arnold's many Planet Hollywood franchises to take their place of honor next to fellow survivors from other films. The production has spared no expense: Three bars, four buffets and two dessert tables; free disposable cameras for snapshots and farewells; presents from the production in the form of *Last Action Hero* hats and T-shirts; special presents from Arnold in the form of sportswear; an elaborate dance floor; and games for the children (after all, this party is rated PG-13). Over in one corner a giant television screen shows a special party video assembled by the film's videographers, alternating shots of the crew with shots from a silent studio tour film from 1925. Apart from the people, very little has changed since then. More than a century since the first motion picture camera was patented, movie making is still the art of alchemy: the transformation of fantasy into a pure light that can be shared with the world.

Arnold Schwarzenegger holds up a microphone. "First of all we want to thank Columbia Pictures and all the executives who agreed to the tremendous budget for 'The Big Ticket of 1993.'

"I want to say that I only meet ten percent of you people throughout the shooting of the picture because you work in the background. You're building sets, you're organizing stunts and so on. A lot of people I don't ever see. But I wanted to make sure that everyone was invited to this party to make sure that we can

all celebrate together. I want to thank all of you for your great dedication and for your hard work. We all know how hard it is to work on a picture for five months. It takes endurance and dedication and you men and women had both. I want to thank all of you and I hope that we do it again soon!" The room breaks into cheers and applause. Arnold hands the microphone over to McT who is reluctant to accept. "Our great director!" urges Arnold. The crew cheers more. McTiernan has to accept.

"I would like to specifically second his sentiments about thanking all of you. I'm sorry we couldn't make it a hundred and fifty day schedule, but maybe next year." There is more applause. After a few more words McT hands the microphone back to Arnold who leads a spirited but off-key chorus of Happy Birthday for production executive Barry Josephson.

As the evening winds down it is as if the entire production is riding off into the sunset, trailed by a slow and old fashioned fade-out. Monday morning, there will still be odds and ends to shoot as well as mountains of work for a small army of sound and picture editors to complete under the pressure of an intimidating deadline. In less than ten weeks the idea Zak Penn started playing with in his mind over three years ago will be ready for the world. A rocket will launch, carrying the film's title into space. Tremendous advertising and marketing will tantalize moviegoers everywhere. Arnold will begin yet another of his intrepid publicity juggernauts that will carry him to cities around the globe.